# The West Coast Trail:

## *One Step at a Time*

By
Robert J. Bannon

A "One Step Outings" Publication
Calgary, Alberta
www.onestepoutings.com

**contact:**
www.onestepoutings.com

ISBN  0-9739646-0-X

Second Printing: 2006
Printed in Canada

Book design & layout by Acorn Communications Inc.,
Calgary, Alberta

Photos courtesy of Heather Compton, Calgary, Alberta

*"Underlying the beauty of the spectacle there is meaning and significance. It is the elusiveness of that meaning that haunts us, that sends us again and again into the natural world where the key to the riddle is hidden. It sends us back to the edge of the sea, where the drama of life played its first scene on earth and perhaps even its prelude; where the forces of evolution are at work today, as they have been since the appearance of what we know as life."*

*Rachel Carson*

## FORWARD

Parks Canada sends out a map to those who've registered to hike British Columbia's West Coast Trail — a forty-seven-mile odyssey that makes most lists of the top ten hikes in North America, both for its stunning scenery and its sheer ruggedness.

On the front panel of the map, before you trace the trail through remote coastline and ancient rainforest, you'll find a sentence that reads, "The West Coast Trail is recommended for experienced backpackers only." Notice that it doesn't say "experienced campers or hikers," but rather "backpackers."

Who knew there was a difference?

Not me. At least, not before I embarked on the seven-day backpacking trip from Port Renfrew to Bamfield on the southwest coast of Vancouver Island. Not before I gained a new appreciation for the word "rugged."

The West Coast Trail. Long before I left for the trailhead with my backpacking partner, Gord Strandlund, a friend had told me that hiking the WCT was harder than childbirth.

As a male arriving at midlife, I can't compare the difficulty between the WCT and childbirth, but I can say it ranks very close to the birth of my two children in creating a sense of awe and a belief in a higher power.

When Gord and I hit the trail, I was questioning many of my beliefs – belief in that higher power, belief in my self, my purpose, my limitations…in short, my raison d'être.

When we completed the trail, I was physically battered, exhausted, dehydrated – and more alive than I had been in years.

The West Coast Trail is located in a temperate rainforest that receives in excess of 150 inches of rain per year. That's more than 12 feet of precipitation – and it's the most influential characteristic that overshadows the preparation, training, planning and actual walking of this trail. The rainfall has carved out ravines that must be crossed or climbed, it provides the juice that spurs the tremendous vegetative growth that obscures, hinders and falls across the path, it is the lubricant that, when added to soil, creates mud, mud and more mud, and it is the reason why backpacks are heavy with extra clothing and supplies.

Hikers are constantly climbing or descending wooden ladders, most on very steep inclines, while carrying fifty pounds on their backs and a walking stick or two in their hands. The slippery and occasionally missing rungs extend up more than a hundred vertical feet in places, but can feel like a thousand.

Mud is a constant whether it is raining or not. In some places it will suck a hiker's boot down so far that it flows in over the top; in others, it creates dangerously slick conditions. Mud-coated roots — encountered daily — call for extreme caution. The rainforest grows big trees with roots to match, and so climbing up, down or over this writhing, treacherous, python-like mass is something that must be endured whenever you're hiking under the rainforest canopy.

Backpacking the West Coast Trail is the hardest thing I've ever done – and the most challenging, most exhilarating and perhaps the most satisfying.

That's because the trail is so much more than a walk in the woods or an escape from everyday life in the city. And it gets experienced on many different levels.

When I was a young man, I assumed – as so many others in that age group did, and continue to do – that I would get to do and see and experience everything again if I wanted to. Consequently, I rarely stopped to smell the roses, watch the sunset, or taste the cool, damp air of the forest. I was so eager to do and accomplish and complete everything, that I didn't take the time to thoroughly experience it. I thought it was more important to get to the end of the trip than to enjoy the journey.

"I would always have time to do that later," formed my credo. There was no need to delve into the greater meaning of life – I was too busy rushing through it and accumulating as much as possible in the way of possessions and experiences. We sometimes treat life as a contest – he who accumulates the most wins. Ah, the arrogance of youth.

And yet, throughout our lives, we are presented with Choice Points. These often show up as some sort of crisis in health, money, relationships or career. They are sent to get our attention and to give us the chance to make a course correction. I had ignored most of them, and so my "course" continued to lead me to something less than I knew was possible.

I didn't feel that I was living up to my potential, and yet spent as little time as possible actually considering my own role and responsibilities in creating the life I was living. I had allowed my life to unfold as if I had no control over it. Rather, events and circumstances dictated whether I was happy, sad, successful, joyful or peaceful.

And then came Day Three on the trail. The more I consider that particular twenty-four-hour period, the more I realize that life is a product of our thoughts, nothing else: we are what we think we are. Day Three is probably the reason I wrote this book in the first place. In fact, it's likely why I undertook the experience of a lifetime to hike the West Coast Trail. Mid-life – I couldn't ignore the Choice Points any longer.

Thousands of people have completed the West Coast Trail over the years, and I would venture to say that each experience has been unique. Yes, the common threads of physical beauty and the opportunity for inspiration will unite them – but the result of that inspiration reminds me of snowflakes: each one composed of the same elements, and yet completely unique.

Day Three occurs to all of us from time to time, whether it's on or off the trail - the chance to delve deeper, to confront our fears and to discover our own individual truth. Those opportunities had happened to me previously, but I had always ignored them. The WCT, however, got – and held – my attention.

I hope the reader will take the opportunity to look at my "Day Three" and perhaps wonder about their own. Do you need to hike the West Coast Trail to find this place? No, but doing something slightly beyond our level of comfort is often the time and place where opportunity and change converge. This particular journey has opened up a world of possibilities to me, and it is now my intention to explore them.

My sincere hope is that each reader will discover some of the possibilities that exist in their lives, as well.

## ACKNOWLEDGMENTS

This book, quite simply, would not have occurred without the support, encouragement, dedication and love of my wife Leanne. For all of that and for her sense of purpose, her loyalty, her determination, insight, intuition and sense of humor, I remain eternally grateful. My kids, Andrew and Tori, continue to teach and inspire me and, in return, I hope they know that they fill my heart with love forever.

To my friend, partner, confidante and foil, Gord Strandlund: even if I had known what I was doing at the beginning of this trek, I could not have joined up with a better person to travel the West Coast Trail with. To both Gord and his wife, Brenda, thank you and good luck as you travel future trails. And I would be terribly remiss if I didn't mention the contributions of Gord's daughter Christy, who so generously offered me her backpack to use on the hike – I hope I didn't stretch the waist belt too badly.

My friend of several years, Bob Meadows – another faithful supporter in so many ways – eagerly offered his sleeping pads and one-burner stove to our venture: our stomachs, wallets and backs thank you.

I have known Kerry and Howard Parsons for more than twenty years, and they have always provided inspiration and support without judgment. The Odyssey Program that they have created, and still facilitate, continues to give me insight and guidance as I go forward on my various journeys. My hope is that they will continue to create connection and reveal truth to those of us committed to the trip. My prayer is that they, and everyone else mentioned, will always experience fulfillment, peace and love.

## INTRODUCTION

As with many truly Canadian stories, this one started in a Tim Horton's coffee shop. Gord and I still can't remember whose idea it was originally, but we both agreed and then verbally committed ourselves to hiking the West Coast Trail. I suspect neither of us really believed we would go through with it. It started as two guys yakking over coffee with equal parts of idle dreaming and bovine excrement. After we both agreed that it would be a great adventure and that we should do it next summer, we spent lots of time talking about it. We shared our thoughts with each other, our wives and then some friends and co-workers, and before we knew it, we actually had to go ahead with it!

We began by buying one of the many books written about how to hike the WCT, which included planning, equipment, menus, etc. Then we rented some videos that scared our wives, and consequently the male ego kicked in and we realized that we'd put ourselves into a position where we couldn't possibly back out.

It wasn't all that hard to find advice on equipment, however. Magazines, countless books (not this one), outdoor equipment stores and people who had hiked the trail before were all eager to provide recommendations for backpacks, boots, stoves, sleeping bags, sleeping pads, water filters, tents, clothing and other equipment. If you decide to seek this information, make sure you tell them where you are going to hike, because it really does make a difference.

Because, of course, all of that equipment, plus food and water for a week, must be carried for the duration of the hike. Aye, now there's the rub. Literally! If you use lightweight materials and equipment along with powdered food, the average weight on a hiker's back is fifty-five pounds. If you're not "experienced" at carrying this weight for long distances, over rugged terrain in the rain, wind and mud, then a life-altering experience awaits you.

That's precisely what we were looking for – a life-altering experience – and I'm delighted to say we not only found it but survived it too. Of course, the process of preparing for that experience raised dozens of questions every day. Was I ready for the challenge? Could I step outside of my comfort zone? Could I set this goal and achieve it? Would I, once again, allow someone, something or some circumstance to dictate my actions and results? Would I get close and then stop? Would I be fit and ready in time? Would I be one of the eighty people per year that get flown off the trail by air and sea rescue?

Some of these questions were answered during the lead-up to the event. Some were answered during the hike itself. Most of the big questions weren't answered until much later, as I began to realize and appreciate what had been accomplished.

At the preparation stage, however, after a few months of research, more talk and thinking about the physical fitness level required, Gord one day asked me when I was going to start a training program – was I serious?

I was fifty-four years old, 245 pounds, had a bad back, worn-out knees and sore feet, and had been a pretty good football player – forty years ago! So, what's the big deal? We had targeted the last week of August for the big event and I was beginning to plan the victory dinner in Victoria.

Fortunately for me, it didn't take a genius to see that I had to do some serious shaping up, which included losing weight and building strength and endurance. In looking back, I wouldn't trade a moment of training, preparing and hiking for anything. Did I say training? Okay, so there are a few moments I would trade for clean, dry shorts and a tube of A535. However, I probably attained the minimum level of fitness required to successfully take on the West Coast Trail, and that in itself was reason for celebration.

Gord joined an athletic club and started working out under the tutelage of a trainer, while I opted to create my own program. I don't think there's any right or wrong in this, but I'm just naturally cheaper (some enlightened souls may add stubborn). I prefer to think of myself as a frugal individual with a strong sense of independence. I figured that we would be doing a lot of walking in order to complete a forty-seven-mile hike, and so with that keen insight, I decided to begin my training program with walking.

I often parked my car near the end of the row, farthest from the shopping center doors to avoid tight squeezes between cars. This provided a walking workout and kept me in tiptop shopping shape. Since I rarely carried much weight into the stores, however, it dawned on me that something more rigorous might provide better results.

I live within a couple of blocks of Fish Creek Park in south Calgary. This 3,300-acre provincial park within the city limits is full of relatively easy hiking, jogging and biking trails. I began by walking to the park and back, completing a circuit of three miles about five times a week. This was combined with a twenty-minute daily stretching program that I found in an article in Men's Health magazine. The article combined the fitness element with a diet that was supposed to increase testosterone levels – so naturally, I went on the diet too. I've always considered this one of God's many jokes. He overloads us with testosterone in our late teens and leaves us wanting in our mid-fifties. Perhaps, He (but more likely, She) could even out the supply-demand curve a bit – just asking.

In late winter, I realized that I was walking past a large set of wooden stairs that joined a busy roadway with an elevated subdivision. This was more like it. We knew the trail featured significant elevation changes, and so it made sense to incorporate some of that in my training schedule. The stairway contained eighty steps, and so I started by repeating the climb and descent (one circuit) five times, gradually building up to ten circuits. This accomplished a number of things. It stretched out my leg muscles, increased my strength and endurance, and provided a great cardiovascular workout too.

As the winter turned to summer, I started to put on a backpack and gradually added weight by putting plastic bottles full of sand inside it. By the end of the training period, I alternated between walking the ten circuits with weighted pack and running the 800 stairs everyday. My body weight dropped about twenty-five pounds and, frankly, I hadn't felt that good in years.

The company I work for, CSS Office Furniture Systems Service, is a significant contributor to the Cancer Kids to Camp golf tournament that takes place in Calgary every August. I had also been telling people at work about my daily stair climbing, so it wasn't too difficult to accept the challenge from Jennifer, our administrative assistant, to put together "Bob's Psychotic Stair Climb." I succeeded in climbing about 1,800 stairs one noon hour, and with funds from my employer to match the various pools and sponsorships that the other employees supported, we were able to donate $3,000 to a great cause. I didn't go out and do my nightly stair climbing on that occasion – I seem to remember that I was in bed pretty early.

Gord and I took two brief practice camping trips to check out equipment and food, and to decide who would sleep on which side of the tent. This in no way actually prepared us for the backpacking experience of the West Coast Trail, but – combined with the physical workouts – provided a minimal level of fitness and knowledge that served us very well. As it turned out, we relied on it every step of the way.

## ON THE ROAD

Standing on the beach, gazing along the shoreline we would begin hiking in the morning, I couldn't completely identify all of the feelings that swelled my heart or gurgled in the pit of my stomach. We were actually here, feeling a damp chill in the evening air, and hearing the sound of waves lapping the shore while seagulls called out in their distinctive chalk-on-blackboard voices. Sand rubbed between my toes as I reviewed the past two days, and the breeze carried the scent of salt water.

Full of high spirits, we had left Calgary late on Thursday morning. We had a reservation on the 9 p.m. ferry sailing from Tsawwassen to Swartz Bay, and about nine hours in the car to go over any details that still needed consideration.

We gave due consideration to the chocolate chip cookies my daughter Tori had baked the night before, and made an executive decision to test them before adding them to our backpacks. When Gord had picked me up in his car, we'd put the bag of cookies (about three dozen) on the back seat, for security reasons, rather than in the trunk with the camping gear. A quick stop to pick up coffee, and we headed west on the Trans Canada Highway. We quickly put work behind us, recorded long term absence messages on our cell phones and shared the support each of our families had offered – and, of course, the cookies.

There was no more training to do, equipment to buy or borrow, customers to call, e-mails to answer or opportunities to bail out. We were on the road to adventure!

We drove through Canada's first national park, Banff, paused in Lake Louise for gas and coffee, and drove on into beautiful B.C. By the time we arrived in Golden, we were beginning to tire of cookies, so we made a quick stop for a burger and began to take notice of the amount of smoke in the air.

In the summer of 2003, British Columbia was suffering from near-drought conditions. Acres and acres of timberland were burning, people were losing their homes and livelihoods, and news reports were showing evacuations in Kelowna as newly built subdivisions fell to the flames. We used my binoculars to look at fires that were visible from the highway as we sped through the Shuswap region and west to Kamloops, one of the major fire sites.

Gord and I could sense the feeling of loss in the choking air, and while we could accept it when nature starts a blaze, through lightning, it seemed like a violation against all of us to learn that some were set deliberately and others by cigarettes tossed by our fellow drivers. Another stop for coffee in smoke-filled Kamloops, and soon we were heading down the Coquihalla Highway to the Fraser Valley.

Once we passed Hope, we could feel a noticeable change in the air, even through the closed windows and air conditioning. I don't know if it was the latitude, the change in elevation or the proximity of the sea, but there was an obvious shift in the atmosphere as we ourselves shifted from highway travelers to woodsmen. We both remarked on it as we drove farther away from work mode, toward this feeling of connection with nature.

It had been a very long time since I had been to southwest B.C., and I was completely dependent on our road maps to navigate us through Surrey, New Westminster and then on to the Tsawwassen ferry terminal, south of Vancouver. We felt the need to hurry, but had made incredibly good time and found ourselves arriving so far in advance of our reservation that we were able to board the 8 p.m. sailing.

We paid our fees and were ushered directly on to the ship, quickly locking our car and making our way to the upper decks. The ship got underway immediately and left the lights of the Lower Mainland behind as we headed out into the Strait of Georgia for our passage to Vancouver Island. Calm water and warm evening air allowed us to go out on the deck and enjoy the salty breezes. By the time we reached the Gulf Islands, darkness had arrived and so we watched the scattered lights appear, twinkling, from the cabins on the islands.

When I'd lived in Victoria two and a half decades earlier, I traveled the ferries so frequently that I had allowed myself to become bored with the trip. Many times I had actually stayed in my car and slept, rather than drink in the experience, as I was so eager to do on that particular night. The sky cooperated, giving us clear horizons and a sail under the stars to Swartz Bay.

We docked just before 10 p.m. and followed the traffic out of the terminal and south toward Victoria. We didn't expect to have much difficulty finding a motel, and so hadn't made a reservation. We were right and easily found a room in Sydney for the night. Unfortunately, there was no restaurant open nearby, so we grabbed some junk food from a corner store and settled into our room to watch the late news.

The TV anchors devoted a lot of air time to the fires in the Interior, interviewing many people who were being evacuated from Kelowna. We learned that a total fire ban had been put into place across the province, and so expected that might affect our ability to enjoy a nightly fire on the trail. We retired early and looked forward to spending Friday morning in Victoria before heading out to Port Renfrew in the afternoon.

On Friday morning, I awoke first, showered, and went across the street to McDonald's for coffee. I had time to read the morning paper and generally acclimate myself to the slower pace of the Island. A slight haze hovered in the sky from the fires, but the weather forecast in the newspaper for the next few days looked pretty good.

I returned to the motel, and Gord and I checked out and headed south for the short drive to Victoria.

I had this overwhelming feeling of familiarity, nostalgia and the sense of returning home as we drove down Douglas Street to the Empress Hotel and over to Victoria's Inner Harbor.

We had time for breakfast and then some sightseeing, and enjoyed a walk around the harbor before driving to Ogden Point for a latte and then motoring along the waterfront of Beacon Hill Park, through the quiet, older neighborhoods of Rockcliffe and Oak Bay. By this time, I had fallen head over heels in love with Victoria again. There is a very appealing genteelness to the city, and absolutely eye-popping scenery, especially for someone who had spent the past couple of decades as a flatlander.

It's funny how some locations have the ability to create joy, ease and peace for me. Even now as I think of the southern tip of Vancouver Island, I can feel that same sense of connection fill me – a warmth and expansiveness that comes direct from my heart.

Gord knew of a place that promised a great lunch, so by late morning we hit the highway to Sooke, en route to Port Renfrew and the trailhead. We tried to find the correct battery for Gord's camera at a drugstore, but to no avail – consequently, we would have only my camera for the trip's duration. Mothers Restaurant became the next stop, for a home-cooked lunch as delicious as Gord had predicted. Busy with locals, it's a spot worth eating at and I have done so a couple of times since.

Lunch finished, we started driving up the road again, enjoying the view along the Strait of Juan de Fuca with the various ships sailing through. The winding, twisting two-laner also passed large reforested areas and the occasional bed and breakfast. The excitement was building as we pulled into Port Renfrew at mid-afternoon and found the unassuming Parks Canada office where we needed to register.

The attendant confirmed our reservation for the following day and suggested that we attend the mandatory orientation session that was beginning shortly, thus allowing us to get underway first thing on Saturday morning. This made sense to us, so we waited around and joined a group of about ten people in the cramped quarters for a discussion of what we might find in the days ahead. This included a warning about a campground closure due to cougar activity and a detailed explanation of how to use the tide tables. If I get a chance, I might want to listen to that last part again someday, as by then my eyes had glazed over with anticipation. The consequences of that would show themselves in about forty hours.

It was pretty apparent that Gord and I were easily the oldest people in the session and, I'm just guessing here, maybe the least experienced. That aside, we were provided with a map and some other brochures, along with up-to-date tide tables and warnings about what to do in the event of injury. It seemed we wouldn't have to worry about that, however, because – according to Parks Canada – an injury required three people: one to be the injuree, one to go for help and the third to stay behind for comfort. There were only two of us, which left no one to be the injured party of the first part.

And besides, we'd signed a release form relieving the population of Canada of any potential lawsuits. I wonder if they also provide a lecture on naiveté?

Once again, we didn't have specific plans regarding where we would stay the night. There were several motels and campgrounds in the area, and it was pointed out that one such camping area was immediately adjacent to the Parks Canada office. We walked over and decided this would be a good opportunity to find out how to raise the tent we had rented from the University of Calgary – and it was a lot cheaper than a motel.

We picked out a site, backed the car in and started to pull equipment out of the trunk. We realized that this would be a lot easier than on the nights to follow. Mostly, we realized that all the equipment and supplies in the trunk would have to be stuffed into, or tied onto, our back packs, otherwise it wasn't going with us. It gave us the ideal opportunity and excuse to finish the chocolate chip cookies. In retrospect, they would have been great on the trail, too!

Setting up the tent went easily, as we found a relatively flat spot among the trees and placed the sleeping pads and bags inside. We had passed the Lighthouse Pub on our way through Port Renfrew and decided to return to it for some libations and dinner. We drove over, found a table in front of the big-screen TV and enjoyed the football game, the local banter of the regulars and our last deep-fried meal for a week – fantastic fish and chips. One of the local fishermen had brought in a big plastic bag full of halibut fillets caught earlier that day, and we thoroughly enjoyed the spoils.

We checked out the view of the harbor and looked across the water at the heavily forested coastline and wondered about what lay ahead. It didn't occur to us that we were looking at the next day's trail and campsite.

We returned to our tenting spot, where we each spent some time on the beach kicking sand and getting mentally prepared for the next day. As we turned in for the night, neither of us realized how all seven senses were going to be awakened and needed during the week to follow. Seven senses? you ask. Yes, seven! Touch, taste, smell, sight, sound and the sixth sense, intuition. And finally, perhaps the most important sense that any of us have and the one certainly needed in the coming days: a sense of humor.

## Day One

Although a fire ban existed across the province due to the forest fires we had witnessed the day before, it didn't appear to mean anything at this campsite, as there were fires galore. This caused Gord and I some concern, but it didn't look as though we could do anything about it. Anyway, after we'd figured out how to set up the tent, we could at least savor several cups of stove-brewed tea before turning in at about 9:30 pm.

Inevitably, at midnight, I felt the call of the wild. It was a familiar call that seems to increase in frequency with cool air and advancing years. Gord and I were lying side by side in our zipped-up sleeping bags and I didn't want to disturb his slumber, so I did my best to crawl out of my bag and the tent in the dark. There should be some sort of training course available somewhere for this, because I felt like a bull in a china shop. Groping in the dark for a flashlight and boots, I was intensely aware of keeping my hands on my side of the tent. Of course, as a middle-aged, highly conservative male, crawling out of a sleeping bag in my underwear brought new meaning to the words "anal retentive." (Not to mention the unsettling nature of the word "groping.")

I sat up and found my flashlight in the side pocket of the tent wall, put on my glasses so I could see the darkness more clearly, and began unzipping my bag. I did my best to remain noiseless but between the huffing, puffing, grunting, groaning and zipping, I'm sure it sounded like feeding time at the zoo. Speaking of zoo, after locating my boots at the foot of my sleeping bag, I needed to escape our cage through the mosquito netting and then the tent door, both closed with zippers. When the tent has a center height of four feet and the aforementioned escapee has a height of six feet, all of this must be done on one's knees. Add darkness, one hand holding a flashlight, a lack of coordination, cramped quarters, well you get the picture – you may have seen those old Martin and Lewis movies, too!

I stumbled through the opening and rezipped the door to keep the warmth inside. I used short bursts of my flashlight to locate the bushes skirting the edge of our campsite and proceeded to find relief while holding the flashlight between my teeth and hoping it wouldn't drop down into the dirt at my feet. It didn't, but after retracing my steps and all the procedures for re-entry, I decided that tea late at night was now a thing of the past. I don't know if my tentmate was just being polite by not saying anything or if he really didn't wake up, but the snoring on my left side halted long enough for me to get back to sleep. Inside every cloud is a silver lining...

We got up early, about 6 a.m., and started packing up. After rolling up our sleeping pads and bags and with great difficulty pushing them back into their stuff sacks, it was time to repack the tent, which came complete with a fly cover to protect the structure from rain and dew. Wilderness hikers are always advised to test and check their equipment before heading into the back country. We hadn't, of course.

What we should have done was set it up in the backyard back in Calgary and drenched it with a garden hose a few days before leaving. That way, we would have discovered any leaks or seam problems and corrected them. We ended up lucky, because we didn't encounter any horrific and very frequent rainstorms during our week. I should add that we placed a lot of confidence in the University of Calgary Outdoor Program equipment rentals – we were lucky again, because the trust didn't appear to be misplaced.

It's a fact that when tents and sleeping bags are manufactured, they are rolled and compressed by huge, heavy industrial machines in a factory before they are mechanically jammed into their carrying bags. This explains why you and I, mere mortals (not those gods of the wild that some backpackers are,) find that only half the tent fits inside the sack – the balance hangs out the end. This allows the previously mentioned gods and other campers to determine who the forest virgins are.

After much re-rolling and brute force, I managed to cram the tent back into its nylon bag, only to discover that we still had a very damp fly cover to deal with. We stood in the clearing, each of us holding an end, and spent a few minutes vigorously shaking the large piece of nylon to try and dry it out. We performed this flapping ritual every morning on the trail, for two reasons: first, the moisture would otherwise spread to the tent if it was rolled up with the fly cover, leaving us with wet sleeping facilities for that night; and second, since moisture could not escape the stuff sack, it would add considerably to the weight lugged on my back for the next week. It took about seven days to actually get efficient at repacking the fly cover, tent and poles into the bag provided and find a way to balance it with everything else in my backpack.

We found a restaurant open for breakfast and took our last opportunity to use civilized flush facilities. We would remember that experience fondly as the days passed and our meals passed along with them. We left our car at a recommended spot at Port Renfrew, run by a nice couple that have been doing this for about twenty years. We threw our backpacks in the back of the owner's pickup and he drove us to the ferry where we would catch a ride to the trailhead. The trailhead was located on the other side of the Gordon River mouth, and so a small aluminum skiff with a wooden bench running lengthwise down the center was used to transport hikers and their gear to and from.

What a great spot! The guy that was running this operation had saved everything he'd ever touched over the past two decades and it was all spread out on his lawn. The result was a fishing gear, washing machine, lawnmower, building material and sporting goods emporium complete with a driving range. In the middle of the yard, overlooking the dock, an ancient golf ball driving mat sat on a beat-up wooden platform, with half a dozen golf clubs and assorted balls completing the picture. Across the river – about 175 yards – hundreds of abandoned golf balls rested in the mud. I'm sure there were more hooks than slices given the propensity for fishing in the area.

We arrived about 8:45 a.m. and had to wait about a half hour for a group of ten from the University of Calgary Outdoor Program to arrive, since they were scheduled to cross and start the trail at the same time as us. We were readjusting and tweaking our backpacks when we noticed the boats coming down the river and heading out for a day's fishing. Now, this wasn't just a couple of motorboats – it looked like an armada as boat after boat, in a line that stretched for twenty minutes, slowly chugged by.

These were good, honest sports fishermen: nine in the morning and already a can of beer in every hand. It reminded me of the movie – the name of which escapes me – that showed this huge fleet of pleasure craft leaving the shores of England during the Second World War to rescue stranded soldiers in France. With my perverse sense of humor, I wondered if I should pick up one of those golf clubs and start winging balls across the channel. That would have scattered the formation and upset a few beers and who knows what else.

Shortly after 9 a.m., a vehicle pulled up and disgorged nine women and one man, the troops from the U of C. We all crowded onto the boat, shuffling equipment and standing shoulder to shoulder and wondering what we'd find just ahead of us. The ferry started up and took us across the inlet and up to the trailhead – a trip of about five minutes, after which we pulled onto a rough gravel beach with a lonely signpost announcing the West Coast Trail.

Most people prefer to finish at this spot, but we'd decided to cover the most difficult section first, while we were fresh (we're still looking for the easy part). We all spent several minutes adjusting backpacks, checking water bottles and taking pictures for each other as we passed a multitude of cameras back and forth. The large group that had landed with us looked as though they were fit, experienced and generally knew what they were doing - we only thought we did!

After a few more adjustments, and stowing our camera and maps, etc., it was decided that Gord and I would strike out first. So, on went the backpacks, our clumsiness excused by the fact that our packs were the heaviest they would be for the duration – or was it the limitations of age and flexibility? Sacrificing grace for brute strength, we left the landing area, stepped past the signpost and waved goodbye to the group that we would see most evenings at the various campsites. We began walking, along a gravel path that lasted for about thirty seconds.

The "path" halted abruptly, and we were straight into old-growth forest: narrow, ever-steepening paths, and tree roots that would be our constant traveling companions for seven days and 47 miles. The trail was obviously a myth. In its place was a physically grueling slog up slippery slopes crisscrossed with tree roots and fallen logs. Within minutes, we were coated in sweat and wondering if we had taken on way more than we could handle.

Maybe we should have started at the other end, but in hindsight, we both agreed that we'd made the right choice – and that we wouldn't trade our experience for anything. I think the male ego kicked in from time to time, too, as the going got tougher and we heard the light-hearted feminine laughter behind us. We were here and we weren't going to turn back – besides, there was no bus route heading back to the trailhead, so we simply had to keep going.

On numerous occasions, we would stumble or slip as we learned to balance the load on our backs and adjust for this changed center of balance. (Perhaps it would have been a good idea to have spent more time training on hard terrain with fifty-five-pound packs.) But the idea of taking one step at a time, and simply moving forward with our complete focus on the next foothold, was beginning to gel.

Added to the physical challenge we had taken on, the beauty, the serenity, and the spiritual dimension of the forest that we had entered overwhelmed us. Breathtaken in the physical and metaphysical sense, we could feel the power, the challenge and the almost sacred mystical quality of hiking the West Coast Trail. We knew we had made the right decision, and that the potential for a life-changing experience was spread out before us.

The rainforest exudes a dampness that you can taste and a smell like no other. The decaying tree stumps, the huge ferns – all green and lush – present an olfactory experience that truly connects us with the natural world in a unique way. The moisture seems to swallow sound, and the size of the trees conjures up the feeling of walking through a cathedral.

On this part of the trail, an old telegraph cable – and, in some spots, a thick steel cable – is visible along the walking path. It makes you wonder at the work required to bring in some of that old equipment and haul it up from the water through the trees. Later, we would see some of the steam-powered machinery that had been left behind.

It's safe to assume that there has been a trail of sorts along this coastline since the introduction of animals to the island. Man followed and would have used the trail for hunting, and gathering fuel and food, as well as for communications between villages or campsites. In modern history, communication was achieved through a telegraph line strung between Carmanah Lighthouse and Victoria in the late 19th century.

But the West Coast Trail also owes its existence to the lethal storms that this area of the Pacific has earned a reputation for within the seafaring community, going right back to the earliest European explorers – the storms themselves, of course, predate these interlopers by several million years.

As ships foundered on the rocks, survivors would wade ashore and attempt to make their way south to safety, but many perished due to the impassable rivers and ravines that dissected the thick rainforest. Starvation and exposure to the wind and rain that howled in off the ocean would bring an even higher death toll to these sea-borne tragedies. It's estimated that more than sixty shipwrecks lie just offshore, some of them still visible at low tide.

In the very early 1900s, following the sinking of the SS Valencia and the loss of 117 lives – many from hypothermia on the shoreline – it was decided to create a lifesaving path. As we were beginning to see, evidence of the telegraph and rescue efforts, along with relics of several logging operations, remains visible beside the trail to this day.

Occasionally – as we stepped deeper into the trail and its stories – we took a quick break for a couple of handfuls of trail mix and a drink of water, but we felt compelled to make haste to the campsite. This turned out to be a recurring theme and a mistake. Hikers beware – stop often and allow your body to rest. We only needed to cover about three miles that day, and no matter how challenging the terrain and heavy the pack, we should have realized that we had lots of time.

In fact, time took on an interesting dimension for us, because we were at the mercy of tides, weather, fatigue and fresh water sources. If we hiked the West Coast Trail again, I think we would simply back off from our concern about those limitations, and trust the experience and ourselves more. We had started at the trailhead at about 10 a.m. and had loads of time to get to Thrasher Cove, our first campsite.

We learned later that some groups skipped this section and convinced the ferry pilot to take them directly to Thrasher. What a shame to miss this challenge and experience. For groups starting at the other end of the trail – without the option to skip this part of it – this is a pretty tough ending, especially if it's raining. The saving grace for those groups is that their backpacks are at their lightest and they are now trail-hardened.

We had been warned in the various trail guides and websites about the difficulty of the trail's terrain, especially on this stretch. We took the warning a little too lightly and found that first day to be pretty rugged. The path has been worn through the years by countless hikers, and probably four-legged animals as well. It has not been smoothed, paved or civilized in any way that would be out of sync with the natural surroundings.

Having said that, the Parks Canada people have created some very innovative ways to make it possible to traverse this wilderness coastline using everything from ladders and swinging bridges to ropes and cable cars. As I think back on it, I can't imagine how adventurers, residents and those many shipwrecked survivors made it through this old telegraph route prior to Parks Canada taking over the West Coast Trail. The constant elevation changes on very narrow, very slick pathways made for very slow going. It was physically exhausting for a middle-aged, lightly experienced but heavily laden man to use twisting, gnarled tree roots to make his way up a steep slope.

Mud and water coated the bare roots, and we found that we had to plan each individual step to avoid falling down or twisting an ankle. Handholds were few and far between, and we had to rely totally on our walking sticks for support, balance and sometimes leverage to help push our tired butts and legs up to the next root. Speaking of legs, it was amazing how tired they became as I dragged each one, step after step, over, through, under, around and across this trail as they burned from the unfamiliar weight load. I began to look back fondly on the 800 dry, stable and repetitive stairs that I had been climbing during what I thought was preparation for this.

Every once in a while, one of us would have to stop and so the other did as well. Without taking them off our backs, we would rest our packs on a stump, take a few swigs of water and a small munch of snack bar or trail mix, and spend a few short minutes looking at our surroundings. This is what we had come for!

As difficult as it is to translate into words the physical challenge we faced with the heavy packs and treacherous pathways, it is even more difficult to accurately convey the timeless beauty inherent in the sights, sounds and scents that we were marinating in. A photograph can display the scene in a one-dimensional way, but only a gifted artist could do justice and interpret the deeper feeling of being on this part of the Earth.

The half-light of the forest floor was interspersed with shafts of sunlight that penetrated the openings of the tree canopy. It felt like a stage, with various plant life illuminated by spotlights on a soft surface of decaying vegetation. The air, still and thick, filled our nostrils with the clean, damp, unhurried oxygen mix that supported life on the planet. We encountered many trees, six to eight feet in diameter, that had fallen across our path and had gaps cut through them with a chain saw so we could stay on the trail. Sometimes these enormous logs became the pathway as they provided a crossing over ravines and streams. Maintaining your balance on a sloping, water-soaked log while carrying fifty-five pounds of gear can be a little tricky, but we made it.

Frankly, we considered those first three miles over rugged terrain that took us from sea level to 700 feet a great accomplishment, and we were ready for some R & R on the beach. That meant that we had to return to sea level, to locate our campsite at Thrasher Cove. It was time to find out about the ladders as we climbed down one after the other, and made our way along slick, narrow paths, descending the entire 700 vertical feet over the distance of about two-thirds of a mile.

The trail boasts dozens of these ladders, ranging from a couple of rungs to some behemoths that are thirty to forty rungs high, with maybe three to four sets of them in vertical groups clinging to cliff faces. I used to own a residential painting business and had an idea of what ladders are like to climb – but my concept was vastly different than the reality encountered on the West Coast Trail. Now, make no mistake – without these ladders, it's hard to imagine how we would have managed the incredible elevation changes from sea level to trail and back again.

But, while we were grateful for them, they also became somewhat of a nightmare. Most of the time, the ladders are straight up and down, rather than on an angle, and are attached to the rock face by all sorts of innovative means. Since they're made of wood – and in a rainforest, dead wood always wants to revert to its original elements – the rungs and uprights are in a continual state of decay. This accounts for the fact that there are often missing steps, along with others that are loose and ready to break without warning. This could be pretty tricky, especially when we were descending the ladders and couldn't see what was below our feet, proceeding almost by touch. If we didn't "touch" a rung, we kept descending to the next one and hoping that it was there and would hold our weight. The rungs on these ladders are spaced farther apart than for normal ladders, and it's no small feat to ascend and descend a series of them with a heavy pack on one's back and a walking stick in hand.

We were thirsty, hungry, tired and thankful as we emerged from the arduous descent to a sandy shoreline that opened onto a panoramic view of the same bay that we had gazed at the night before from the mouth of the river at Port Renfrew. We felt that we had traveled to a different time zone, but we were looking across the water at the small town where we'd eaten dinner just twenty-four hours earlier.

There were two guys in place who had already set up a tent, and we proceeded to find and stake out a site just down the beach from them. The beach was loaded with logs that created areas of ownership, like fences in the city. We found a great location, with driftwood surrounding it and a few flat pieces that served as a cooking counter and backpack shelf. Fresh water flowed down a creek that cut through the sand to the salt water, and a few deeper pools allowed us to use our water filter and refill our bottles. It didn't take long to get our tent up and then throw our sleeping bags, pads, etc. inside, with the sun warming both us and the sand at our feet.

We soon had fresh water, and took a few minutes to sit and watch an eagle soar along the shoreline above the treetops. More hikers gradually began arriving from both directions, setting up their own campsites. Along with a great feeling of camaraderie came respect for people's space and their desire to enjoy the experience.

We took the opportunity to get our stove going, and made Mulligan stew from a package of powder and lumps. I later made a note that I'd had an extra helping because I knew I needed the nutrition; however, five-star dining it wasn't. The powdered food mixes use lots of spices to create the illusion of taste.

I remembered our camping experience at Dinosaur Provincial Park a few weeks earlier. Our overnight trial run had included cooking on a one-burner stove for the first time and following the package instructions on one of these gourmet delights for our dinner meal. Gord had added a spice package to a pot of cooked noodles and mystery meat, and while eating this tasty treat, we both noticed some hard, black granules that were pretty gritty on the teeth – apparently spice chunks that hadn't mixed properly. Now, it should be noted that I wear glasses full time, but Gord only wears them when he wants to see. As it turned out, Gord's spice package was actually some kind of dehydration chemical compound to keep the powder dry. We only made the mistake once, but there's no way I'm going to let him forget it. I assumed most of the cooking duties from that time, while my tentmate did a great job of keeping everything clean and neat.

We cleaned up dinner pots, bowls, etc. and made tea. Then we perched ourselves on a log, finding it both peaceful and exciting to be drinking the restorative brew, watching a couple of fishing boats jockey into position in the bay, listening to the water lap at the beach, and seeing the various groups arrive and set up camp along the shore.

We thought we had snagged one of the better sites to camp on, but really, we were all setting up our tents on the sand with the same view of the water in front of us and a backdrop of very high, tree-covered cliffs behind us. We watched our friends from the U of C arrive and begin pitching their five blue tents right at the beach access in front of the outhouse and bear-proof food locker. Camping on a salt-water beach has a unique beauty of its own and for those of us who live our landlocked lives experiencing water from rivers, lakes and taps, the ocean water changes position on the beach constantly.

The tide revealed incredible beauty as it moved out, and awesome power as it carved out caves and surge channels along the trail.

The tide becomes a significant factor in planning a West Coast Trail trek. It determines not only where you pitch a tent on the beach, but also when you leave camp if you want to hike along the ocean instead of in the trees. It's also a tremendous demonstration of how the natural world controls us instead of the other way around. In our arrogance on this planet, we sometimes think that man is in charge. We are only the top of the food chain - nature makes the big rules that we ignore at our peril. One of the little blue tents ignored the high-water line, and had to beat a hasty retreat to higher ground when the water threatened to overtake its inhabitants.

Since we were not looking forward to climbing up all of those ladders to regain the trail the next morning, walking the beach at low tide seemed a possible alternative. We consulted our maps and tide tables, and determined that if we left about 6:30 a.m. the next day, we would make the next beach-to-trail access point prior to the high tide that could leave us stranded.

After dinner I walked up the beach and around a point out of sight of our camping area, and discovered a beautiful stretch of white sand strewn with rocks and tide pools. This looked like a great alternative to reclimbing those ladders.

I came back to camp after an hour of solitude, and Gord and I agreed that we would leave early in the morning and take the beach route. During the evening, I overheard one guy, who had just come in from the north end via the beach route, say to his friend that it was the hardest thing he had ever done. As I sit here in snow-covered Calgary, writing about our experience, I am still amazed that we survived Day Two.

## Day Two

Up at dawn, and Gord was first out of the tent and already packing gear. The two men who had set up camp just prior to us the day before were getting an early start as well. They planned to reclimb the ladders and take the forest route. We were anxious to get started on our beach alternative, and so began a pattern of skipping breakfast in order to get moving. Gord was substituting power bars, and I settled for trail mix and a full water bottle. We headed out around the point that I had scouted the night before, with our backpacks loaded and hockey sticks in hand.

I haven't mentioned the hockey sticks before, but since there is no question that mine saved my life every day, including this one – both literally and figuratively – perhaps I should talk about it. My son, Andrew plays hockey, and consequently I have a garage full of broken or outgrown hockey sticks. Now, I hadn't done much hiking in a long time, and I'd never really considered a walking stick or hiking pole. However, the books we'd read all suggested one and sometimes two, and the various camping and outdoor stores we'd visited all had displays of high-tech, ergonomically correct, lightweight schussing systems – glorified ski poles in my mind. The whole idea smacked of commercialism, or at least the prices certainly did.

Neither of us gave the idea much thought, but at the last moment decided that maybe we should look into it. We had sometimes fashioned walking sticks from felled branches discovered on our various preliminary hikes, and I was ready to admit that they'd served some purpose. Besides, call me Don Cherry, but if I run into a curious cougar or a belligerent bear, I want a good sturdy piece of Canadian hardwood in my hands, not some composite material, left-wing, over-priced, politically correct trekking pole system. So, we cut down a couple of hockey stick shafts and threw them in the trunk with our gear, almost as an afterthought. Thank God!

During our first day, the hockey sticks helped provide stability on wet surfaces and occasionally prevented us from stumbling or tripping on the ever-present tree roots. Sometimes they just gave us something to lean on and take some of the weight from our backpacks. We were soon to discover their value as a significant safety device, however; in fact, as far as I'm concerned, mine became the staff of life (saving).

We moved down the beach, enjoying the early morning trek along the sand, sidestepping occasional boulders and logs and checking out the tide pools for signs of life. We kept our eyes peeled on the water in search of any signs of whales. On our right-hand side rose high cliffs that were obviously impassable and so the map we were using was correct – no trail access until we passed Owen Point. We also noticed a growing number of boulders on the sand. They increased in quantity and size until, after half an hour, we could no longer avoid having to climb over them. These boulders spend about half their time covered with seawater and so have lots of algae and other growth clinging to them. This makes them treacherous to climb and walk on. Combine these slick surfaces with knife-sharp ridges carved by the movement of water and sand, and you have the beginnings of what the map described as "a difficult route" and what we'd overheard the night before as "the hardest thing I have ever done."

Some of these boulders were bigger than apartments I've lived in. Their horizontal surfaces were littered with smaller rocks of all shapes and sizes, a testament to the unbelievable power of the ocean. Imagine if you will, this jumbled mass of teetering boulders, incredibly slimy, with traction provided by jagged-edged footholds that were never flat but sloped in a thousand different angles and sizes. Mix the boulders with chasms of tidewater of countless depths and sizes, and logs long stripped of bark by the stormy seas and tossed throughout the scene like spaghetti dropped on the floor from a box. Now add a hiker that only imagined that he knew what he was doing, challenged by a lack of nutrition, still physically tired from the day before, overweight, out of shape, with a fifty-five-pound backpack that has changed his center of gravity. On that morning, it became a lethal cocktail.

Constantly stepping over (sometimes jumping) crevices of various widths and depths, struggling to maintain balance, slipping, falling, scrambling, trying desperately to find handholds – cut hands, elbows, knees, shins banging rocks. The idea of "one step at a time" was never as sharply defined as during this stretch, which took every ounce of strength and energy, every morsel of my determination and focus.

No time for whale watching, picture taking or navel gazing – this felt like survival at its most basic. Sweat burning my eyes, using the hockey stick to provide support and hoping it wouldn't slip because there was no place to land that wouldn't result in injury. Find a place to put one foot. Move to it. Find another place to move the other foot – move, repeat, slowly, feel the muscles strain, catch myself sliding, jam the hockey stick into a crevice – halt the slide. This stretch of hell took about forty-five minutes to complete, and managed to create the defining moment of the week – and one of the defining moments of my life.

Without warning, I found myself perched atop a huge rock with my right foot on an angle pointed down and twisted away from my body. About four feet away, my other foot was wide to the left and angled toward the ocean on a different boulder. In between was a channel of inky water of indeterminate depth. The rocks created a very steep angle, with sand, pebbles and sharp ridges – shiny with brine and aquatic growth – all pointed down to the boiling liquid about three to four feet below me. The pack on my back had shifted so that my center of gravity was, in fact, perfectly centered – I couldn't move. I gingerly waved my arms, seeking further balance or a non-existent surface for support, but I felt like a tightrope walker with no safety net.

I couldn't shift my weight to move forward; my left foot was too far out in front to allow me to move backward. I was in serious trouble and my muscles were screaming for a decision, but I could not move. I knew that I was at perilous risk of an injury such as a broken leg or ankle, or a serious face plant into those sharp ridges. Gord was far ahead and didn't know the predicament I was in – I needed help! But where would I find it? I'm not kidding – my stomach lurched, and a wave of anxiety washed over me.

Was it a miracle? I don't know – maybe. Some sort of inner calm came over me. I've never experienced anything like that before. Rife with desperation and fear, I absolutely felt the prayers of many people back home. I knew, because several had told me before I had left, that they prayed for our safety. I just knew that I needed those prayers at that time.

A couple of deep breaths and a glance skyward produced no chariot drawn by white chargers, so I guessed that I'd better figure a way out of this predicament. I looked down at the boulder between my legs and noticed a small indentation about eighteen inches below my right foot on the face of the rock. When I say indentation, I'm talking about an area the size of a saucer and probably the same depth – a place to put my boot?

I looked at it a couple of times. It meant lifting my boot and letting it drop down to this minor indentation, and praying that my foot wouldn't slip further. If this crease in the rock didn't hold, there was no way I could stop myself from falling down into that black water to an unknown fate. My weight plus the pack and gear meant about 280 pounds going down onto one boot, trying to hold its position on a greasy dimple of rock face. I couldn't find any other alternative and I was tiring fast. This was a moment of truth. I had to trust and have faith, not in myself but in something completely beyond my control. Flashing through my mind were thoughts about God, prayer, trust, fear, family, and air and sea rescue operations.

Letting my foot fall down this eighteen-inch step was not a controlled function – there was too much weight behind it. I let go and my heel slammed into the rock, slipped a bit and miraculously held. This was a tenuous hold at best and I was actually deeper into the hole than when I'd started. I had to make the next step almost immediately with the same leg, lifting up about two feet to another foothold. Remember high school physics? A body in motion tends to stay in motion. It's true.

It was nothing more than faith that got me moving. If I had broken my leg and had to be flown out to a hospital, we would call it misplaced faith. But because it was successful, I get to wonder whether it was faith in God, faith in myself, or faith in the power of some Universal force beyond my understanding. Writing this, many months later, I'm still not completely sure about how faith works or what exactly I had faith in. One thing I am absolutely certain about – faith is what moved me forward, nothing else.

I was out of immediate danger, but as I wended my way over ever more boulders, an unpleasant odor started to assault my nasal passages. These mountains of rock covered everything from the water line to the smooth cliff faces that extended up to a crown of tall trees and bush. The only alternative to scrambling over them would be to head out to sea and swim. On the other hand, some creatures swim in from the sea and get caught in this maelstrom of basalt and seawater. I heard Gord yelling at me from way up ahead to look out for the seal skeleton. That was the smell, a rank odor carried on the ocean breeze to us hikers and, Gord was convinced, to the bears in the region, too! I saw the skeleton caught between the rocks – nothing left for any bear.

Onward over the boulders, and eventually they started to thin out and patches of sand began to show. This gradually gave way to a great stretch of white sand littered with rocks and logs, and a veritable cakewalk compared to what we had just covered.

We spent some time exploring a cave carved out by centuries of storms and tides, taking pictures and a well-deserved break. A good thing too, because challenge number two for the day was almost upon us.

Much of the beach along the West Coast is made up of dark, black rock. When you find a stretch of it, it's like walking on a sidewalk with ridges, sand, gravel, algae, tide pools and something called surge channels frequently cutting through between the water and cliffs. Surge channels can be six inches across, a minor curiosity to step over, but they can also be a few feet across, tempting to jump or find a log to bridge the banks. Some can be rampaging channels of surf, impossible to attempt in any conditions.

These channels have been cut out by the constant movement of waves, tides and storms – a true example of the immense power of natural forces. They create just one source of awe on this majestic coastal trail, and witnessing the evidence of the raging seas helped to explain the many shipwrecks in this "graveyard of the Pacific." It also created a sense of place for ourselves, making us at once miniscule and at the same time magnificent in our ability to appreciate it.

Our cave was at beach level, part of a large point of land that cut off the beach and forced hikers to approach the seaward side when the tide was very low. We needed to get around this point – Owen Point – in order to continue our hike and eventually find a beach access that would lead back up to the trail through the forest.

We walked out on to the rock shelf, only to find a large and obviously deep surge channel blocking the route. Now, some of the books talk about crossing through these channels on foot. The idea was to remove our boots and put on sandals or go barefoot. We would have to take off our backpacks, hoist them over our heads and wade through to the other side. This presented many misgivings for both of us. How deep was the water? How slippery were the rocks below? How would we climb down into this channel and back out the other side? Neither one of us was keen at all. They were named surge channels because the water, driven by wave action, really does surge in and out. Frankly, this wasn't an option.

So – we couldn't move forward. There was no trail access, either on the map or obvious to us, without retracing our steps back over those damn rocks – no way! Running up from the beach, however, was a smooth, sand-colored cliff face on which we could discern a very narrow ledge about twenty feet above our heads. This ledge followed around the point, but we couldn't see where it went beyond that. It looked as though we had no alternative but to try to reach the ledge and see if it presented an option.

We needed a way to scramble up the cliff face to the ledge, so we took off our packs and found a slender vertical crease that looked like a possibility. Gord started up first, grabbing the straps of his pack and lifting it up in front of him, setting it down and taking a step or two to follow it. It was slow going on this steep slope, which was covered in fine sand, making it very hard to gain ground on. I followed behind and we gradually made our way up to a ledge no more than a foot wide. No grace involved in that little escapade, but grace of a different sort would be needed soon.

With no room for either of us to move around, we couldn't get our backpacks up onto our shoulders. We had to turn our backs to the cliff and side-step, because there was not enough room to do anything else. We continued to shuffle, crab-like, along this pathway to see where it led. With our backs to the cliff, we had a nice view of the ocean spread before us and could even see a whale in a kelp bed off the shoreline a few hundred yards out. It was hard to enjoy the sight from this precarious perch, however, so we kept inching along the cliff, until we could see that the path was about to dead end. Now what to do?

We were clinging to the side of the cliff, trying to find something to hold on to, keeping our backpacks from falling over the edge by leaning them against the rock face. We noticed an old piece of nylon rope, frayed and faded with age, a loop tied in it, hanging down from above us. The loop was about five feet above the ledge, so we could reach it, but we couldn't see what it was tied to or where it might lead.

A senior level management meeting was required. We had more risks to assess and decisions to make. Once again, we had no alternative other than to retrace our steps, so really, no decision to make. Somehow or other, we would have to attempt to climb up this rope, ever higher on the cliff and ever farther from the sea-lashed rocks below. I had very little trust in that piece of twine. It looked like a leftover from one of the original shipwrecks. The strands were fraying, the color bleached and it wasn't very thick to begin with.

My buddy, the little guy, said he would try it first. We were able to reach the rope with our hands, but it was a long, I mean long, step up to get our foot in the loop. After that, we had to find a way to grab the rope and pull ourselves up, hand over hand, in order to even see what to do next.

I held onto Gord and guided his foot into the loop as he lifted his leg as high as possible. I needed to provide a brace for him so that he could get up without tumbling backwards off this little sliver of a path. I managed to push him from underneath – no picture available of this maneuver, thank goodness – so that he reached the rope above his boot and pulled himself up while I provided a hand from below. The rope didn't break as he found another foot loop above the first one and finally had some leverage to power himself up the slope. He disappeared over the top and continued to use small trees and undergrowth to find handholds and eventually reach the top of yet another sharply angled slope. Only then was he able to disentangle himself from that forlorn length of rope and stand on terra firma.

When Gord went up, he took a length of rope with him from our supplies and tied it to the sturdiest tree he could find. That was harder than it sounds, because these were all small trees holding onto a thin layer of soil and trying not to blow away during the ocean gales. The next step was to get the backpacks up to the same level Gord was on, so he threw the rope down and I tied his pack to it.

We couldn't see each other because he was back about ten feet from the edge, standing on a steep pathway that sloped toward me and the twenty-foot drop from there to the rocks below. Gord was actually about another twenty feet above me, and fortunately the rope was just long enough to allow him to pull the overburdened backpack up through the rocks and dirt. The rope came back down and I tied my pack on and watched as it scraped and bounced up the hillside, leaving me stranded on my thin little wedge of cliff face, wondering.

We had packed some quarter-inch polypropylene rope at the suggestion of one of the guidebooks, but being the penny-pinching person that I am, I bought it at a discount store, thinking we would only be using it to tie up tarps and clotheslines. We were about to put it to a much bigger test.

Here we go with faith and trust again. I thought I just had that lesson an hour ago! I'm about fifty pounds heavier than Gord and I didn't like the look of that old piece of rope that we had to climb up on. What were the chances it would hold me? Gord threw the other rope back down to me and shouted to tie it around my waist. This would be interesting – I flunked knots in Boy Scouts and always buy slip-on shoes for a reason. Not to put too keen a point on it, but I was about to tie a knot that my life, as I knew it, might depend on. Then I was supposed to figure out how to raise my foot high enough to shove my boot into that loop on a piece of rope that looked older than me. Gord had tied the other end of our rope around his waist, and expected to be able to hold my weight if I slipped or if the other rope broke.

This is sometimes known as an "oh shit" moment. Life seems to be like that. We go through periods of tranquility and ease, then through times of fear, hard work and struggle, and then get confronted with "oh shit." The solution is the same. First faith, then trust, then a deep breath and step out into the abyss. That's a lot easier when there's no other alternative, but I wasn't thinking of that at the time.

The benefit of looking at this through the rear-view mirror of time is that I didn't see the scene behind and below me. I was reviewing this sequence of events with Gord the day before I wrote this – several months after the fact – and he just informed me that, at the time, he'd been hoping I wouldn't see how high we were and how far I would drop to the rocks below. Apparently he was as fearful as me. Good thing I didn't know it then.

In order to get my left foot high enough to reach the rope loop, I had to trust that the second rope tied around Gord would hold my weight as I leaned back into space. The next move was to swing up, into the loop and pull myself up onto that rope. Somehow this was accomplished and the loop held, as I used plain old brute force to leverage and step into loop one while using that motion to keep me moving up to loop two with my right foot. So far so good and with those two large steps, I was about halfway up the cliff and could see Gord struggling on the sand-eroded path, trying to hold me.

I heaved my boot into another loop quickly, and was able to grab a handful of underbrush. This took some of the weight off Gord and gave me more leverage, even though the brush was pretty loosely rooted. One more step into the next loop and I could swing my leg up onto that dusty, slippery pathway. I grabbed onto some more bushes and kept pulling while Gord took up the slack on the rope and continued to drag me. Once again, no grace exhibited here, but fear of falling is a great motivator. Scrambling, covered in dirt and sweat, I clambered up to Gord's feet; he grabbed my shirt and I was safe!

Out of danger from the surf and rocks, we sat down and surveyed our surroundings. They consisted of trees, fallen logs and underbrush – this little pathway we had crawled up to led nowhere. We took a few moments to rest and figure out what to do, and then checked and sorted out our backpacks after the pull up the cliff. We tightened and double-checked the various items that had been tied onto the loops and straps. Everything secured, we found ourselves about forty feet above the shore on a rocky promontory with a curtain of trees shielding any route inland and an incoming tide starting to cover our tracks below us.

It didn't look good, but we knew the general direction in which to head, in order to find the trail. If we kept the water at our backs, then we would have to eventually bisect the trail by bushwhacking. This meant pushing our way through this coastal undergrowth, trying not to get ourselves, our clothing or equipment snagged on the vegetation or stumble over any fallen trees. Our visibility was virtually zero as we hacked and slashed our way forward in search of open space. Going through both of our minds was the fear that we could literally stumble across a cougar or bear. We made no secret of our presence as we talked loudly, constantly banging and crashing while surveying our immediate surroundings in search of safety.

Eventually we could see over the growth as it started to thin out and the big trees once again began to dominate the landscape. We knew we were moving in the right direction to intersect the trail, and so we persevered until at last we found it. We had slogged our way to mile 42, a mere five miles from the start of our trek and perhaps two lifetimes closer to discovering the possibility of the real life we sought.

We were back on the trail and heading through the forest toward Camper Bay, which was still about three miles farther on. Boardwalks covered some of the boggy areas, and we used fallen logs to bridge other mud holes. Since this was a very dry summer, I can't regale the reader about the quantity of muck we encountered, but can only imagine what it would be like during a wet season.

Gord was once again eating a power bar for fuel while I satisfied myself with trail mix. Neither one of us felt like stopping to unpack all the gear and find the stove in order to make soup or something hot. In retrospect, it may not have made the best sense nutritionally, but from a practical point of view we should have planned and packed for cold lunches instead.

Perhaps it's different with large groups or with people who have hiked the West Coast Trail more often, but the whole idea of stopping at noon and preparing a cooked lunch still doesn't seem to make sense. We had followed the instructions in the various guidebooks and planned hot meals for lunches, but for the second day in a row decided against it. When you're exhausted from the physical effort that we had experienced, a couple of things happen: first, you don't feel particularly hungry at the time; and second, you don't always make the best decisions about nutritional, liquid or rest requirements.

Of course, at the time, we didn't recognize this as an issue. We tramped on without further incident, both lost in our own thoughts and the enjoyment of the rainforest and occasional glimpses of the ocean. We still marveled at the vegetation, the scents, the quiet and, I think, at the fact that we were really here and had survived a couple of very demanding days.

At about two in the afternoon we descended from the trail down a few ladders to discover Camper Creek and our first cable car. The creek was really just a trickle, so we opted to use the rocks in the bottom as stepping stones to cross to the camping area to find a site for our tent.

Camper Bay is well named, as the creek empties into a large beautiful bay with views across to Cape Flattery on the U.S. side of the Juan de Fuca Strait. We found a site beside the creek near the trees, in front of the "Beware of Cougar" sign. We were well above the high-tide mark and had some shelter from the tree canopy nearby in case of rain. We had a nice big log to act as a privacy barrier, wind shelter, clothes hanger and cooking counter - all the comforts of home without the constant conflict of who controlled the channel changer.

We both had to get out of our boots and relax for a while after getting the tent set up. This allowed our boots and socks to be placed on the log for airing. It was too early for dinner, so we spent time yet again going through backpacks and equipment. We noticed the two men we had met the night before already here with their gear set up on the north side of the beach, closer to the water. They probably had a little better view, but there is no such thing as a bad view on the west coast of Vancouver Island. I went for a walk to do some exploring while Gord continued going through the equipment and supplies, sweeping sand out of the tent and generally staying busy.

The water from the creek had created a couple of pools that bordered the tenting area before making its way to the ocean. A hump of sand and rock had built up between these pools and the salt water, acting as a natural barrier to rough seas. This seawall looked like a great place to find a seat and simply watch the waves roll in, so I set out over the gravel beach and tiptoed through the shallow freshwater pools.

It's easy to feel that human life originated in the ocean, because we all seem to be naturally drawn back to it. There is a rhythm to the waves that feels in perfect harmony with our spirits and the natural beat of our bodies. I find it hypnotic and incredibly riveting, powerful and yet very natural. Like most people, I get lost in watching and hearing waves lap the shore. I sat on a log for about a half hour, allowing this time and place to soothe my tired mind and relax my body. The tide was low and this later gave me the chance to walk north from our site along the rock shelf and look at some fabulous tide pools. If you observe closely, they teem with aquatic life. Starfish, mussels and amazingly green underwater plants create pictures no television screen could ever reproduce.

The cliffs on either side of the bay entrance were about a hundred feet high and exposed the layers of time for all to see. It's amazing that so many of us seem to have trouble getting a plant to grow in our house while out here, trees sprout from the most improbable crevices in sheer rock. The ocean has carved out caves and sculptures that create a gallery to honor nature at its most spectacular. This wasn't preplanned, organized or artificial in any way – it was absolute raw beauty.

Against an overcast and cool afternoon, with a freshening breeze off the ocean, people were starting to arrive from either end of the trail and set up their tents. There are no organized or delineated campsites, but people just naturally try to respect their fellow travelers and allow them the space to savor the West Coast Trail experience.

I was beginning to experience hunger pangs, so I started making my way back down the beach to return to our tent. Gord had decided to enjoy the beach and tide pools as well, and so I snapped a picture of him when I saw him gazing out to sea. He joined me as we looked at the entrance to a cave that could have been fun to explore, but was impossible to enter because of the intensity of the water rushing in and out. I headed back to camp as Gord continued up the coastline I had been exploring.

More people were arriving all the time and so things were getting busier and more crowded, but we had picked a terrific spot. We had fresh-filtered water and a dinner that seemed a little better than the day before, as far as I was concerned. Hunger helped us appreciate the powdered food, but a fresh apple or banana would have been better than the heated blueberry glop we had for dessert. We made tea again, washed up our dishes and ourselves, and discussed our plans for the next day.

Soon the five blue tents from the U of C group went up in front of us. We learned that they had assigned group meals to two different people for each night, and that they had a gourmet repast complete with after-dinner drinks planned for tonight. Surprisingly enough, we didn't even try to invite ourselves. It was starting to become dusk and after the day's events, the idea of crawling into sleeping bags became more and more appealing.

Just as we were closing down for the night, another group of about ten students showed up and pitched their tents right beside us. They told us that they had started from the trailhead on that same morning! So it took us two days to cover what they'd had the energy to do in one day. They also had the energy to cook dinner in the dark, filter water for the next day, set up tents and pass around a bottle of liqueur. Once again, we declined to join the party – aging was sure beginning to make me feel old. After the exertions of the day, sleep came quickly and soundly.

## DAY THREE

Writing is an interesting process. For the most part, I have physically written this project in chronological order. I started with Day One and did some brainstorming, made brief notes of my memories of that day and its events. Then I sat down and wrote out my recollections of the hike longhand. Each day seems to revolve around specific experiences that occurred to us, or things that we saw. Generally this technique has worked pretty well and over the past few months I have tried to contribute to this book on the basis of a little bit each day while maintaining my family life and a full-time job.

The exception to this technique is Day Three. It seems to be a blank spot in my memory bank. This hasn't been just the result of the several months that have passed since the hike or even the ravages of aging. I couldn't remember Day Three on the day we finished the trail. I don't think I remembered Day Three on Day Four. I know for certain that on our drive from Victoria to Columbia Lake following the hike, Gord and I reviewed much of our trek, except for Day Three. It seems to have disappeared down the rabbit hole. To date, I have simply pushed on and continued to write about the following four days with the intention of returning to this one when I was finished, but the thought has been a source of worry. Did this mean I would have to make up the day or would my mind finally release the thoughts and events to my pen?

I don't give her enough credit but sometimes – okay, most times – my wife is very wise. She would like me to edit that to read "wise beyond her years." Please consider it done. When I finished writing about the final day on the trail, she knew that I had been struggling with Day Three for some time. We stopped at a Starbucks for coffee one morning, and I was expressing my trepidation about the next writing step when she said, "Obviously, the most significant part about Day Three is your lack of memory. That should be the focus of your writing."

Well, of course, I could have figured that out…eventually. Shortly afterward, I was talking to my friend Kerry and expressed the same concerns to her. She, too, is very intuitive and insightful, and has a knack for asking just the right question. "What about the connection between your memory loss and the original purpose of hiking the trail? Is there something to say about that?" she asked.

To say that I have forgotten everything about this day is not exactly accurate. I have retained bits and pieces, visual pictures and overall impressions. Specific sights and some trail features rekindle themselves through a review of guidebooks and videos.

An explanation for this memory gap seems fairly easy, at least on a physical level. I was exhausted at the time, on a level that I probably hadn't experienced before. Now, I don't think that happens to everyone, but it did happen to me. I'm tempted to try to write about the deeper, metaphysical and perhaps spiritual, reasons that may draw comparison to how many of us block out certain aspects of our existence to avoid pain, confrontation or change. There may be something to that idea after all.

Keeping in mind my age and physical condition, the previous two days had been a complete and total challenge to me physically, and consequently mentally as well. Day Three was in many ways a repeat of Day One – constant elevation changes. It might be described in one phrase: ladders, rocks, ladders, ladders, mud, ladders, ladders, ladders, roots, roots and ladders.

We packed up and left the campsite about 8 a.m. in a light drizzle and immediately began encountering ladders back to the trail. Climbing to reach a height of about 400 feet gets the day started with a pumping heart and warmed muscles very quickly. The morning became a blur as we found that our energy reserves had been depleted from the previous two days and for some reason it didn't occur to us to seek some rest on the beach until it was quite late in the morning.

A year later, as I look back on this, I realize that most of us, at mid-life, begin to understand that we have done a version of this dance in our real lives too. Plodding, pushing, climbing, ignoring, grasping and then around midway wondering –why? Here we were on Day Three with life in microcosm. It felt like I'd gone full circle in some ways. Back to the reason I decided to hike the West Coast Trail in the first place - to stop and take a look at what was important, to check the view, to smell the salt air, to experience life on a new level.

Instead, I had decided it was more important to get some place, to adhere to a schedule, to forego my personal needs in pursuit of…what? Rather than reassessing and altering the plan, rather than accepting what was in front of us and letting go of an arbitrary set of decisions based on unknown facts, we forged on. In a nutshell, this embodied why I had traveled to Vancouver Island in the first place.

Mid-life had brought doubt about my past and anxiety about the path ahead. It wasn't just the notion that I hadn't realized my dreams. If someone asked, I couldn't have recalled or described those dreams. Sure, I could make up a list of things I wanted - a house on the ocean, new sports car and world travel - all the same stuff everybody says.

The problem was that when I said that, the only thoughts that came to my deeper mind were the ones that said, "You don't have them now, you're not smart enough, not educated enough, you don't deserve those things." Doubts, depression, anger and envy had become my reality. I had replaced my childhood dreams with someone else's version of how I should live - work hard, get a real job, grow up, stop daydreaming: in short, who do you think you are for wanting the impossible?

If you don't think this is a major issue in the world, try the following exercise: Ask a four-year-old what his dream is, what he wants to do, what he wants to be. Ask an eighteen-year-old the same question and then ask yourself or someone in their fifties the same questions. The answers go from childlike joy, wonder and awe to this dejected shrug and a resigned acceptance of what we think is the truth. We have taught ourselves to accept less than what we want in many areas of our lives. Is it any wonder that antidepressants are the largest selling group of drugs on the planet?

There is no comfort in having company in this case. It seems that most of the world is self-medicating on drugs, gambling, alcohol, food, shopping, TV, nicotine, caffeine or a combination of these. Now, wouldn't that make a great reality show?

I had spent many years in neutral. The disappointment of not being immensely successful in business was balanced by the fear of daring to wish for anything too big in the future. Thus I avoided further disappointment. Work-day wise, for several decades I had mostly gravitated to those fellow employees that did the most complaining, therefore finding validation for my own lack of success. It was much easier to blame the boss, the economy, the booze, the government, the customers – anyone or anything to avoid going inside my own self in search of the answers.

While hiking the West Coast Trail was a trip to the outside world, by Day Three it had already tested everything I knew about myself physically, intellectually and emotionally. The inner journey engendered on the trail had, however, begun months earlier, while questioning my life's journey and purpose during the Odyssey Program, led by my friends Kerry and Howard Parsons.

I had long equated success with money, flirting with the almighty dollar from time to time over the years. Mostly, I had observed money from the outside by associating with people who had it. Never feeling on an equal footing with these same people, I nevertheless felt some sort of affinity to both wealth and the wealthy. I have no idea where that comes from, but as a result I always had this strong sense of failure for not having produced wealth in my own right

I had read most of the books about loving money, the law of attraction, the wealthy barbers, millionaires next door, the path to this and the path to that. All of the authors were well intentioned, but I'd always come up short when it was time to put their programs into action. The programs were probably just fine, but apparently I had not been ready, until now.

Faced with a forty-seven mile trek through remote rainforest, survival was based on "ready or not, here I am!" Perhaps it was this sense of immediacy I craved - putting myself on the line and having success measured by survival rather than dollars. No question about living in the moment on the trail, because I couldn't project beyond the next step without risking a missed foothold and a broken ankle. Perhaps this explains our fascination with danger, with extreme sports: the concept of putting it all on the line raises the bar from tracking a financial score card to tracking life itself.

The Odyssey Program had challenged me to consider my past, but more importantly to look inside myself to discover my purpose. In the spirit of "one step at a time," this trail represented forty-seven miles of steps – a wild mathematical projection could see that as 150,000 steps – not including those damn ladders.

Late in the morning, we came upon another creek that emptied into the ocean. Instead of using the cable car, we followed it down to its mouth and an inviting sand beach. As always, the beach was strewn with big weathered logs that provided the perfect perch for an extended break. It was midday and several people had set up campsites upstream on the north side of the creek. Apparently, they had decided to take the day off to enjoy and regenerate. We still didn't get the hint. Gord went off to filter some more water, to replace what we had used during the morning, and I was able to relax on the log and enjoy the sun that had begun to shine.

While I was enjoying this badly needed rest, many people said hello to me as they continued on their own treks. Two people stood out in particular: one was a heavy-built gentleman in his early sixties. He had a European accent and carried the largest backpack I had ever seen. He was heading south to where we had come from, and

I've always wondered how he made out with what looked like sixty-five to seventy pounds on his back.

The second person of interest was one of a group of three or four young guys hiking together. For some reason that I forget, one of them had his own backpack on and another pack, which belonged to a friend, strapped to his front. I think the friend had been injured and flown out, but the remaining party still needed the equipment and supplies in the backpack. I assume they took turns doubling up the weight they carried. In any case, this young fellow had a decidedly grim look about him. I didn't get the feeling that this section of his journey was particularly pleasant or fun – but it was certainly the nature of the experience on the West Coast Trail: awe-inspiring and exhausting all at the same time.

Gord returned to the log with fresh water and we both took a few more minutes for a snack and drink before saddling up. We waded through the creek mouth and I got a soaker as water came in over the top of my boot. Apparently Gore-Tex works great unless you decide to actually pour the water into the boot as I had done. Nothing serious, however, as I'm sure my foot welcomed a little fresh water by that time.

We made our way back up to the trail and set out to travel through the bog area. This region has a very unique look and feel about it. There aren't that many big trees, but the vegetation is incredibly lush as it grows out of this soggy, muddy terrain. As I've said, this was a particularly dry summer and the plant life, exposed to more clear sky, showed it.

It was easy to see that in any kind of wet weather it would be almost impossible to get through the mud. This accounts for long sections of boardwalk that have been built by Parks Canada. This stretch of the trail must have been hell for earlier hikers, and especially for shipwrecked survivors in the early 1900s. It was a treat for us, however, even though we still needed to take care not to break through a rotten board or tumble off into the muck from some of the less stable sections.

We planned to go to Walbran Creek, and managed to get there about mid-afternoon. We found a great spot on the beach (once again, there were no bad ones) and formed a corral from the driftwood and logs to mark our home site. In the process of writing this chapter, my memory bank has released more information. There still isn't the richness of detail that I have come to expect, but that gives me the opportunity to reflect on a different part of the journey.

I needed to up shake my life. By this time, I knew that my body had been shaken up, but what effect was this process having on my life? How had I managed to get myself to this place? I'd had grand ideas before, but something always seemed to get in the way of completing them. I had spent a lifetime of making that "something" look like it lay beyond my control. This entire journey was different from start to finish (if there is a finish).

I had been on a retreat once before in my life, when I was about sixteen. My mother insisted that I spend a weekend at a monastery in Guelph, Ontario. Strangely enough, this teenaged boy seemed to be acting up a lot and needed to spend some time contemplating his life, according to her. I know full well that my mother really, and not so secretly, hoped that I would decide to become a priest. I sure enjoyed the monastery food, the silence and the escape from everyday reality, as it allowed me to read both of the James Bond novels I had smuggled in my luggage. Alas, no priest emerged in my future. I did, however, experience a feeling of reverence then that I've felt several times since, including the times on this hike when the trees that surrounded us seemed to reach to heaven itself.

Retreat was exactly what this West Coast Trail hike was all about, too, as it became a world apart from my usual reality, right from the day I had begun taking it seriously many months before. Somehow, I sustained the dream through months of cold, wet, windy, typically Calgary winter weather. And then, many weeks of sun, heat and more wind through the summer. I sustained this dream through aches, pains, tiredness, work, family and skepticism. The skepticism was on the face of people who couldn't connect the project with the pudgy body speaking the goal; it was also on the face of the guy staring back at me in the mirror every once in a while. The idea of hiking one of North America's greatest trails evoked fear in the pit of my stomach, but there was another feeling there as well - a feeling that hadn't been all that common recently – the feeling of excitement.

*Bob and Gord – lunchtime Day Six.*

*Ladders, ladders, ladders.*

*On the boardwalk.*

*Bridge on the River Klanawa.*

*Beachwood condos.*

*The roots of all evil.*

*Channel surging at Owen Point.*

*Heaven can wait.*

That was the difference. Excitement – a deep-seated excitement that transcended everyday life. This was different from the excitement I felt about a second helping of dessert or a new car or some other toy. This was quieter. It provided strength to my spirit. It was beyond the realm of "I want to do this or have that." Instead, this resonated within my core and my soul. As I trusted the power of the feeling, it led me, directed me and made decisions for me. It was this feeling that took me out of the house on cold, wet nights to run the 800 stairs I was doing every day. This same power gave me the strength to drive past Dairy Queens on hot summer afternoons.

I couldn't have articulated this at the time, because I was too busy living in that moment, but the more I learn from my search and from the hike and all that surrounds it, the more I realize the truth and power of tapping into my inner self.

I had generated something bigger than myself, something greater than the sum of the reasons for not doing it. This truly became my North Star and in so doing, became a concrete example of living life on purpose. It's no coincidence that the objective of participating in the Odyssey Program earlier in the year was all about finding my life's purpose. This became a living, breathing objective that had inspiration, perspiration, soul, spirit and excitement pulsing itself into being. It wasn't the hike itself that began to breathe life. It was me. I had surrendered myself to the feeling in my stomach, and the Universe lined everything up to cooperate. My wife's gallbladder operation, daughter's camp, my health, vacation time, work projects, household bills and repairs - everything lined up to accommodate me in completing this journey.

Does this sound like a big deal? I'm not so sure it is. I think maybe this is the natural course of events when we tune into the power within and trust our feelings. My rational mind, however, wants to create some organized methodology for how this process occurs and how we decide which ideas to pursue. Ideas, I think, are generated in many ways through coincidence, inspiration and desperation. All ideas create some kind of emotion or feeling within us, and recognizing which kind of feeling will lead us in the direction of joy, freedom, peace and fulfillment.

I don't know about you, but I often blew right by the excitement feeling and all too frequently embraced the idea that generated a heavy feeling instead. This was a need-based desperation that often produced a nothingness within me. When I followed that path, it inevitably led to depression, anger, self-loathing and a realization of failure. Too often I pursued ideas that, had I been in touch with my feelings, I would never have followed. Honoring feelings seems to be a life-long pursuit – and a challenge that's all too often ignored. Now, I know that I'm going to be excommunicated from the old-boys' club for even having mentioned this f-word, but perhaps for the left-brained among us I could offer a small chart.

| coincidence inspiration desperation | become an idea *which leads* | *to a* feeling or emotion | resulting in | joy lightness smiles | *or* | heaviness failure depression anger lethargy *"no choice"* |
|---|---|---|---|---|---|---|

**Choose the feelings you prefer**

Just identify the feelings or emotion associated with an idea or thought – sounds too good to be true, doesn't it? So, how do we do that? The answer – be quiet. Yes, that's it, be quiet.

Who knew that the harshly croaked command from parents to kids all over the world, "be quiet!" actually holds tremendous wisdom and knowledge? When you think about the society we have created in the western world, is it any wonder that so few of us are able to identify with our inner selves? Our inner voices could be shouting at the top of their lungs and we couldn't possibly hear them.

We surround ourselves with a blanket of noise from the moment we awake until we rest our heads on our pillows at night and beyond. The morning alarm goes off and the radio automatically turns on. Music and inane disc jockey banter follow us to the shower, and we create more noise with running water, toilets, electric toothbrushes and hair dryers. Then the anticipation of things to do at work, home or school begins to creep into our thoughts. To the kitchen, turn on the TV or radio and get the newspaper, further fill our minds with the horrors of yesterday and the breaking scandals of today. Into the car, turn on the radio for traffic reports and more information, honking horns, trucks blasting by, the anxiety and stress levels rising by the mile.

Unless you're heading to a remote fire lookout to work, I'm guessing you won't experience even a single moment of silence or peace during your day. The drive home repeats the morning crush hour. Then what? The gym, more noise, home, dinner and talk or TV. The inevitable phone calls, visitors, meetings and courses and then we end the evening reading someone's book that tries to solve our problems, or worse, watch the 11 p.m. newscaster's litany of woe and trouble to create the mood for the night's sleep.

At this moment, I'm sitting in a shopping mall writing this chapter. I just got up to use the washroom and purge a gallon of coffee. While standing at the urinal in the men's room, I looked on the wall in front of me to find a TV screen running ads for products and services available from the various merchants. While I'm purposely ignoring this intrusion, two men walk in together to use the adjoining facilities, spending every moment talking business to each other. It would seem that we can't even go to the bathroom to find peace and solitude like my father used to do when he needed to escape my mother's nightly job jar.

If this description comes close to your typical day, is it any wonder so many of us are looking for love in all the wrong places? We keep looking to someone or something else to transport us to Nirvana, to come and save us. The magic pill isn't in the new self-help book or lecture, it's not on the flavor du jour TV talk show, in the new relationship or at the bottom of the bottle. It's in the moments of silence we purposefully create for ourselves. We've been carrying the answers with us all this time, like a backpack through the forest of trees that we call life.

To hear the answers, perhaps to hear the questions, we absolutely need to create a retreat for ourselves. This is a private period of time - private in the sense that it does not include our spouse, best friend, kids or anyone else. It doesn't include a bestseller, a spa, a good bottle of wine or a new CD.

Most of us can feel lonely in a crowd, but to find true peace we can only go within, and be alone. To discover the voice that can speak only truth requires the ability to hear without something outside of ourselves competing for our attention. What we need is retreat. Re-treat. If we assume for a moment that life is meant to be a "treat" in the sense of trick-or-treat, then a re-treat would be a return to this place of treat or delight or joy...or truth.

Hiking the West Coast Trail, while physically daunting, was nevertheless an example of the "treat" that life and our connection to the earth is meant to be. It was like a return to my own spirit self. I would never tell him this verbally, so Gord will have to actually read this book to find out that he was the ideal partner on this trek. He, too, was on a journey of discovery and consequently he not only respected my need for quiet and reflection, he needed that same space for himself. Neither of us felt the need to fill the quiet times with words or noise, and that included the driving and ferry crossings. What a wonderful opportunity to share this voyage with a good friend who respected my need to re-treat.

Since that week on the trail, I have carved out some time each morning for myself, to try to engage that deep inner voice. For me, the time between 5:30 and 6:30 a.m. is my hour of power, or my retreat. No one else is up in the house, there is no radio or TV on, and I leave the newspaper outside until I'm finished. I generally mix up my concoction of wheat germ, flax and cranberry juice, sit in a large overstuffed chair, leave the lights off and do my version of meditation. I typically spend anywhere from five to fifteen minutes with my eyes closed, doing my best to let go of the thoughts that enter my head. I am more successful with achieving emptiness on some days than others, but this cone of silence I wrap myself in feels very much like a gift to myself.

Almost always, a sense of peace and calm overtakes me and sometimes I try to extend that circle of peace to include people and circumstances that are close to me. All I'm trying to do is give myself the opportunity to hear the truth. I follow this with about thirty minutes of reading something inspirational now that my mind has been prepared to receive it in the silence.

There are hundreds of books out there on meditation and its benefits, but one of the constants is the need for a place that creates the right atmosphere. Noise, but mostly busyness, is a huge distraction to fight through in order to hear that inner voice and calm.

Dave Chilton wrote a wonderful book called The Wealthy Barber, in which he proposed that we faithfully take ten percent of our earnings every week and put it into savings. Over our lifetime, this relatively painless approach will result in a vast wealth of dollars. If we were to invest just five percent of our time, about an hour a day, in our spiritual growth, in retreat, I would suggest that the wealth of mind and spirit would be beyond measure. What could happen if we were to create an hour a day of silence, on purpose? How much less stress, improved health, peace, freedom and joy would result from this discipline?

As I've said, I find the space early in the morning for my retreat, but many people can't or don't want to find the time then. They would rather seek this oasis for the spirit at another time during the day – but when? It's hard to do when you're working in an office building, a school, hospital, car, truck, airport, etc.

Funny you should ask, but I can think of a place in every town and city on the continent that is quiet, has low light and almost nobody in the building. This is especially true during weekdays, when so many of us really need to have a quiet hiding place for an hour to purge the various kinds of noise that assault us during a typical day. Where is this place? Church! Every city I've ever been to is overflowing with churches, often surrounded by beautifully manicured landscapes, but essentially big buildings full of quiet. Who cares what denomination it is? Just pick the closest one that's open. They aren't going to ask for your membership card or a secret handshake. Walk in like you know what you're doing, sit down and close your eyes.

I love some of those church smells that remind me of childhood – candles, incense and old wood. This is the perfect purpose for a church building – to provide space for people to get in touch with the truth of themselves. A retreat. A place to find peace, forgiveness, enlightenment. A place to meditate in silence.

As many of us reach midlife, in the dawn of the Age of Aquarius, we seek connection with something that has been present throughout our lives but just beyond our grasp. The self-help and spiritual sections of every bookstore are bursting at the seams as writer after writer attempts to connect us with our own potential. Many of us seek the truth through challenging pursuits that are designed to test our resolve, question our beliefs and open our minds to endless possibility.

By this third night on the trail, I knew I had met this challenge, knew that I could do it again, knew that I had connected with the earth in a powerful new way, and knew that I had uncovered another layer of truth in myself. Gord and I, each in our own way, expressed the sense of satisfaction and the feeling of being one with life that had overtaken us on this hike. On one level, of course, it was exhaustion, but I think we both sensed a deep peace as we fell asleep that night.

## Day Four

The day broke gray with a breeze off the ocean and mist clinging to the trees. We gingerly made our way over the logs to where we had tied our food in the tree the previous night, and recovered our bags of supplies. Some of the clothes that I had washed were still wet, and they didn't look like they would dry much with the fog and cool, overcast conditions.

Washing clothes that are a blend of nylon and cotton is not a great idea, since the cotton retains the moisture and consequently the weight – however, sometimes the clothes leave you no choice. I therefore packed heavier-than-usual pants and socks into a plastic bag and loaded it into my backpack.

We had covered most of our stuff with a tarp to keep the moisture off, but the tent and fly were still pretty wet. Lots of shaking and flapping made it as dry as possible while getting rid of some of the sand that had attached itself, as well. No breakfast on this morning – we had heard that there were hamburgers up ahead with our names on them!

You can walk on a great natural breakwater here when the tide is out, so we decided to make this our route of choice. Walking in the sand may make for great romantic moments, but romance was the last thing on our minds – the draw of real food had more magnetism than anything else. We picked our way up the sharp, slick outcroppings to get to this West Coast "highway," marveling at the line of black, flat-topped rock that stretched before us, protecting the beach on our right from the wild, blue Pacific on our left. We were walking on relatively level stone, but it still held many tide pools, grooves, algae and moss, as well as loose rocks and stones thrown up by the waves at high tide. We still had to take care, and as usual it was one step at a time.

Huge flocks of seagulls used this area of the coast like it was their own, tolerating our interference with much noise and a few missiles dropped on the unwary. Eventually, we had to return to the sand, as the "roadway" disappeared back into the ocean. This wide beach area, bordered by rugged cliffs with a crown of trees in full leaf, rivals any postcard perfection, but walking on it became an art-like experience. We tried to pick out a route that would provide the hard-packed variety instead of the loose stuff – soft, loose sand was almost impossible to walk in for any length of time, especially with heavy packs on our backs. We would just sink in, requiring enormous energy and strength, even over short distances. Generally, the sand seemed harder packed where it spent more time under water, so we were always trying to determine the high-water line to give us a guide.

My partner had a tougher time of it because he has smaller feet (about four sizes), and so he would dig into the sand deeper. I, on the other hand, had much more boot surface and was able to plane across the sand. So, small feet are better for roots and more difficult on sand, while my size thirteen boots were easier on sand and hell on the tree roots. Great, no one told us that we should consider boot sizes in choosing a backpacking partner!

I think we were becoming better acclimated to the physical demands – and the terrain was easier – so even though the weather was cool and damp, it was a nice hike to get the day going. We made good time on this three- to four-mile section along the coast without pushing too hard. We found beached logs from time to time and enjoyed a short break and a drink from our water bottles. Fog blanketed the strait, but we could enjoy the waves as they came onto shore, the raucous call of seabirds (mostly gulls) and the various tracks left on the sand by both birds and animals. Seals and sometimes sea lions congregate on the many rock outcroppings here. Having binoculars makes spotting these colonies easier, providing a great way to enjoy another of the trail's natural wonders. I, especially, welcomed the change from yesterday's slog through the trees.

Continually during the days of trekking, we would meet people hiking in the other direction. Many of them were very friendly and we often stopped to compare notes or offer observations when asked. Remarks about our unique hiking poles were a constant: the word seemed to have spread about these two guys with the hockey sticks, and a number of people commented that hikers ahead of us had told them to say hello to the "hockey stick hikers."

It was getting to be late morning and we assumed that the large, high jut of land in the distance was Carmanah Point, site of the only staffed lighthouse on the trail. If that was Carmanah, then according to legend and all those hikers we talked to during the morning, Chez Monique was just ahead.

Sure enough, tucked back from the beach in the trees appeared a structure of two-by-fours and clear plastic. No neon signs, liveried valets or waiters, no snooty maitre d' or white linen tablecloths, but the large quantity of backpacks, boots and poles littering the front of the building told us we had made it. We were at the entranceway to heaven with an angel standing behind the cash register.

Think of words like oasis, unique, rustic, godsend, lifesaving or ambrosia, and when you combine them, they spell Chez Monique. Easily the provider of the world's best hamburger, Monique actually warned us to only order a single because a double would be too much. Either she was right or my stomach had shrunk, but the burger was huge and absolutely delicious. We both had a couple of Cokes and took a Gatorade for the road. Any chance that we felt deprived of real food? All that nutritionally-balanced powder and lumps was a thing of the past, for that moment at least.

I said earlier that there were no white linen tablecloths. Well, the truth is, there was no floor either. Inside the plastic-covered framing was an odd assortment of tables and chairs scattered about, sitting right on the sand. In retrospect, that only seemed appropriate since we were supposed to be "roughing it." There were no empty chairs inside, so we sat on the patio overlooking the ocean. More mismatched tables, steel chairs and sand floor, but who cared? We were sitting on chairs, not rocks, at a table, not a log, and eating real food, not rehydrated powder. No foil pouch or boiling water in sight. We were about halfway, time-wise, through the trail and enjoying a perfect meal with a view you couldn't buy for a million dollars.

Sitting beside the cash register was a large cardboard box with a variety of items in it, and a hand-written sign attached that said, "If you need food – take it. If you have too much – leave it."

This could only happen in this unique corner of the world. Anywhere else, and some entrepreneur would be turning an obscene profit with this little idea. People, especially neophytes like us, often misjudge the amount of food to take. Some bring much more than they can eat and others don't bring enough. Once on the trail, there are no commercial establishments (other than this one) so if you don't have enough food, or lose it, or it gets wet, or eaten by mice or bears, you're in big trouble. On the other hand, if, like us, you pack two pounds of coffee and don't drink it, and five pounds of trail mix and only need a pound, and you decide that you don't want the various egg-based breakfasts in a bag, then you really begin to hate all that extra weight.

Actually, the word "hate" isn't really strong enough, but since this is a family report, let's say that when long-distance backpacking, you resent and perhaps use colorful language in reference to every single ounce of weight. This "color" is repeated not daily, but hourly. I had the majority of the food in my backpack, and saw an opportunity to unload a number of unnecessary items, all in one fell swoop. It was the fastest I'd moved all morning – into the food bags. Out came unused soup mixes, omelets, desserts, coffee and trail mix, and anything else we knew we wouldn't use, all tossed into the cardboard box. We weren't the only ones who had done this, but the male ego took another hit when a friendly lady looked at us and asked, "Your first long-distance hike?" I didn't care: I figured that I lightened my load by almost ten pounds and it probably cost about fifty dollars – a great deal!

Monique's big dog wandered around, playing with his revolving band of friends, some of whom were enjoying a few adult beverages and swapping tales of the trail. We still couldn't get a seat inside and were cooling off quite a bit while sitting in lawn chairs outside in a chilling drizzle, so we paid our bill. As we got ready to leave, I realized that Chez Monique reminded me of a desert oasis: surrounded by white sand and filled with laughter and stories, the scents of food cooking and the hubbub of people coming and going. It added to the exotic adventure in a Canadian, down-home kind of way.

Packs lighter, stomachs full of actual cooked food and spirits lifted, we set off toward the beach access and a return to the trail through the forest. We found the familiar colored floats hanging in the trees to indicate the trail, and began climbing back up to the forest and along the path to the lighthouse on Carmanah Point.

At the entrance to the well-maintained grounds that surround the lighthouse, several notice boards and displays depict the efforts to change this particular location to an un-staffed, automated facility. Due to the efforts of many people, this didn't happen, and the lighthouse keeper and his family continue to provide the personal service that is a hallmark of all the personnel associated with the West Coast Trail. We were about to see an example of this caring service firsthand.

We spent some time observing the buildings and equipment, as well as the residents' garden, but didn't feel comfortable intruding any further on their privacy. Apparently some people have had tours and been the subject of the keeper's hospitality, but we didn't see anyone outside – so, after enjoying the incredible view from about a hundred feet above the water, we decided to head back to the trail and move on.

During the last two evenings at our campsites, we had noticed a group of about eight people traveling together – three men and five or six boys. This appeared to be a Boy Scout outing and the kids were having a ball in spite of the loud orders barked by the over-zealous alpha male leader. They would set up a variety of tents, tarps and other equipment in an area usually in front of the entrance to the latrine facilities. This meant that the rest of the campers had to balance on logs around their tents and pick a path to get to the privies – not total hardship, of course, but a mild irritant nonetheless. Anyway, that aside, they seemed to be moving at the same pace as us, overnighting in the same locations and creating badge-worthy experiences, I'm sure. They were at Chez Monique during our time there, and one of the boys had apparently expressed the fact that he didn't feel well.

There is a highly cooperative initiative by all those people connected to the West Coast Trail – the Parks Canada staff, air and sea rescue professionals, and the First Nations whose land the WCT either borders or crosses. The Guardians of the Trail take their responsibilities regarding the safety of the land, people, water and wildlife very seriously. To their everlasting credit, they swing into action on a moment's notice and perform heroic deeds to protect the various stakeholders. Examples of the service they provide are abundant, and almost sound routine until you witness their dedication in action. Then, the depth of their caring becomes obvious for all to see.

A short time after regaining the trail from the lighthouse, we saw a young man coming toward us on the run. You never see anyone by themselves, let alone running, and as he got close, he stopped and asked us if we had seen the group of scouts that were nearby. We replied that they'd been at Chez Monique when we left, and wondered if there was a problem. He explained that Monique had overheard one of the boys complaining about not feeling well and feared that he had ingested untreated water, a concern that was treated with extreme urgency. An alert was quickly communicated to the Guardians in the vicinity via radio, because the risk of drinking giardia-laced water can be life-threatening. If this had been the case, air and sea rescue would have immediately flown him out to a hospital for emergency treatment.

Isn't this a terrible comment on how we treat our planet? Here we are in a pristine wilderness on the remote west coast of Vancouver Island and the water here, just like the water around the rest of the globe, has become so polluted that we risk our lives by drinking it without adding additional chemicals to "purify" it. The older I get, the more this upsets me, and I'm not convinced that all the blame rests with big industry.

Each one of us needs to do what is within our own power to protect the Earth. We need to take personal responsibility in cleaning up after ourselves and being serious about our overuse of pesticides, detergents and the other highly toxic chemicals we use every day in our own homes and offices. One step at a time, just like hiking the West Coast Trail: do what is in front of us, take responsibility for the things we have control over every day. I would get down off my soap box now, but I've stopped using soap in a container of that size.

Thankfully, the young man in front of us received a radio call informing him that the scout had been found, and the culprit that caused his queasiness wasn't water consumption but food over-consumption! The dangers of not having eaten real food for a few days: we all risk gluttony and its predictable after-effects. Maybe that's why Monique suggested a single burger instead of a double.

We now had time to chat with this would-be rescuer, and discovered that he was the son of the lighthouse keeper, back home for the summer on his university break. He was deeply attached to this piece of heaven and respected the unique life experience he'd had while growing up here. It seems such an isolated and lonely life to live in a lighthouse, but not to this individual. To him it was home, and rather than reject his history and roots as so many do, he enjoyed returning to them.

So, after a nice conversation, we returned to the trail and on to Cribs Creek to camp for the night. Cribs provided one of the best sources of fresh water to date: relatively deep and running nice and clear. We met a fellow hiker at the water pool while filtering our supply for another night of cooking, washing and tea. He was obviously pretty experienced, and was doing the trail with his wife. We had been having some minor difficulties with our newly purchased water filter and he showed us how to keep it operating smoothly and quickly. The West Coast Trail is full of people like him – eager to help and share and ensure the success and enjoyment of their fellow trekkers.

We again set up in the sand, thankful that we had switched tent pegs back at the U of C when we'd rented our shelter for the hike. Originally, we were given the standard metal pins for pegging our tent down, but they don't hold in sand: the larger plastic ones held everything in place much more effectively.

We weren't that hungry because of the burger, chips and drinks we'd enjoyed at lunchtime, so we settled back to enjoy some sunshine and relaxation while the day's hikers began showing up and arranging themselves among the logs on the shore. Those hockey sticks came in handy again as we set up a make-shift clothesline to hang some of our still-wet clothing to dry.

All of the campsites along the trail have bear-proof boxes to place food in overnight. These are metal and raised up off the ground, with tight-fitting doors. They work very well to keep animals of all sizes from snacking on our food stores. More importantly, they keep animals from being attracted to the tents during the night – not only the big wildlife, like bears and cougars, but porcupines and mice as well. It doesn't take long to realize that the lockers have a finite amount of space, however, and if you don't get your food bags in them early, then you have to hang the bags in the trees as we had done on previous nights. Perhaps it was short-term memory loss, I just don't remember, but we didn't get our food into the lockers in time this night either.

As dark fell, we needed to find a sturdy, overhanging branch that would hold the weight of our rainproof food sacks. When several thousand logs get stacked by the storms that rage on this coast, they tend to be thrown about pretty haphazardly – the key part of that word being "hazard." We were becoming more adept at climbing over them in sandals, even though they can be treacherous from water or sand and always seem to be moving as our weight tipped them on never-ending pivot points. Some of the logs were more than three feet in diameter, but they varied in size down to a few inches. It all added up to a jumble of shifting footbridges better suited to four-legged felines than middle-aged homo sapiens.

Our friend from the waterhole told us about some overhanging trees he had used, and offered to lead us to them in the rapidly approaching darkness. Gord – he of the small feet and light weight – was far more adept at maneuvering these logs than I, but for a much better reason than foot size alone: he had light – I mean real light – attached to his forehead! Does that mean he had "foresight"? Apparently.

Gord had one of those new, high-intensity lamps that attach to your head with a harness that looks like something a miner would use. One of his daughters had given it to him for Father's Day and he was delighted with it. I had seen these things in some of the camping supply stores and dismissed them, along with the hiking poles, as another piece of useless junk. What's wrong with a good old-fashioned flashlight like I had brought along? "It was good enough forty years ago, why not now? . . . yada, yada, yada."

Sometimes you just have to drag me kicking and screaming into the modern world – that is, the one that's spherical instead of flat. The problem with a flashlight is that it takes one hand to hold it, and even my limited math skills can figure out that that leaves only one hand to hold things, move them, grab on for support, unzip or whatever. Yet I'd looked upon these silly little lights on the head with complete disdain and not a little arrogance. Oh well, no fool like an old fool. I'm sure glad I didn't share my feelings with Gord or his family, prior to this, that is.

My hiking partner strapped on his light, grabbed a food bag and followed our newfound friend over the logs, the two of them looking like a pair of trapeze artists with halogen headlamps and unerring accuracy while jumping from log to log. And then there was me - flashlight in one hand, food bag in the other, stumbling, grumbling, bumbling, an example of someone unbalanced…ahem.

I eventually caught up with our two intrepid log rollers as they looked up into some trees to find a branch strong enough to hold our food. These branches need to be fairly high so that a marauding bear can't reach up and grab the rope along with the bag of goodies. Now, to get a rope up and over a branch that is probably twenty to thirty feet above the ground requires tying a rock or small piece of wood to the end of the rope and throwing it up into the tree.

So, there we were: it was dark, and two guys had lights attached to their faces - the light beams pointing to wherever they were looking. They're standing on logs like loggers in a competition, throwing a rock in the air, scrambling to regain their balance, watching the rock and the entire length of rope fall to the ground and then repeating the process. Guy number three finally arrives with flashlight in hand and tries to follow the flight of the rock with the light beam sweeping the branches and leaves. I'm not sure, but I think I saw Larry, Curly and Moe doing something similar on our old black and white TV as a kid. Eventually the rope hung up on a branch that seemed strong enough to hold the two bags, and we tied it off to a tree branch to secure the food supply for another night.

It was time to turn in for that night, since the next day would require the longest distance to be covered to find the next campsite. We would need to travel ten miles, along with a ferry crossing at Nitinat Narrows. The tent sites among the logs were pretty well occupied by now, but as we settled down for the night we watched a line of lights bobbing its way along the beach toward us. With night upon us, it would have been difficult for these hikers to secure a spot among the logs as we had done.

Instead, they began pitching tents on the ridge of sand between us and the waterline. We realized two things – first, this was the troop from the University of Calgary, quite a ways behind us time-wise, but seemingly having fun as their laughter drifted across the beach. Second, those headlights allowed them to pick their way through the rocks and logs, cook their dinners and arrange their tents and sleeping bags, all in the dark. I was beginning to accept the fact that these forehead-mounted beacons might have some value after all. Eventually, I see the light!

It always amazed me how easy it was to sleep out on the trail, despite the snorer on the other side of the tent. There was no newspaper available to roll up and smack him across the nose, but a few well-placed punches during the first two nights created a noise vacuum that allowed me to fall asleep quickly. I don't know if the snoring persisted for the rest of the hike or if sheer exhaustion overwhelmed the noise factor. In any case, the source of noise emanating from within the tent kept any wildlife at bay. I suspect that fear of the size of animal sleeping inside the tent, based on the sound volume, scared away any snooping bears, along with any monsters hiding under the sleeping pad.

On this particular night, we lay in our sleeping bags listening to the waves crashing on the rocks. The tide had come in and so the waterline was relatively close, about 150 feet, and the rollers thundering into shore hammered the natural stone seawall so hard that we had the impression they were about to shake the tent to pieces. When something hits that hard, with the intensity of a locomotive, you expect to feel some sort of vibration. I noticed that night that no vibration penetrated through the sand and sleeping pad, and it kind of left me expecting something more. The sense of expectancy must have been for something else.

I notice this in other areas of life as well. For instance, I have suffered with chronic foot pain most of my life, to the point that I had simply accepted it. When I got out of bed in the morning, I expected my feet to hurt, especially for the first few steps. This showed up on the West Coast Trail, naturally, and in fact, I had some concern over a newer, more intense pain that had started shortly before we left to begin our hike. I didn't share this with anyone and didn't talk to the doctor, just in case whatever I had developed would cause me to cancel the trip. How's that for a brilliant intellectual maneuver? I wonder if there is some connection between avoidance and pain, pain and expectancy, expectancy and space?

When I returned from Vancouver Island, I talked to my doctor about it and after x-rays were checked we discovered that I had arthritis in both feet. Great – don't you just love old age? Several months after this news, I heeded the advice of several people, including Gord's wife, my wife and my daughter, and decided to submit myself to the ministrations of a brilliant reflexologist.

As I write this, I have just completed my third treatment and the difference is nothing short of miraculous. I no longer have pain every time I stand up. I do, however, still have the expectation of pain, so it surprises me when it's not there. We seem to accommodate pain in our lives so readily and resist confronting it and solving it for so long. What is it about humans that we wear pain and suffering like a badge of honor? Letting go of this pain has truly created space in my life, not unlike the space that was created after the waves crashed into the shore and no vibration resulted. Expecting the vibration and not feeling it, expecting the pain and not feeling it, opens up the opportunity to experience something new. In both cases, for me, it was the space to experience peace. And a peaceful night's sleep followed quickly as we enjoyed the dark night and the rhythmic thunder of the waves.

## DAY FIVE

Day Five was already upon us. Who knew what day of the week it was – and who cared? Days on the West Coast Trail are named one through seven, so very little consideration was given to proper names. The trail was supposed to be getting easier each day, but it was still going to be a pretty good challenge to reach Tsusiat Falls, ten miles away, so an early start was imperative.

As usual, everything was fairly damp when we arose, but we got water boiling, had oatmeal and packed up clothes, cooking gear, tarps, sleeping bags and tent. I had started wrapping my sleeping bag in a black plastic garbage bag and attaching it to the bottom of my backpack, which offered convenient straps and clips for this purpose. It allowed for more room inside the bag and much easier access. There would have been room for a second water bottle or a hydration system – something else I had considered but decided against, to my detriment.

This particular stretch of beach, to the next trail access, was owned by several large flocks of seagulls, which used the beach and air space as they saw fit (and they can't even read a tide table). The rock shelf here provided many opportunities to enjoy tide pool life, but we were in a hurry that day and decided to head back into the forest and make tracks. Besides, we didn't particularly like the look of the tracks this flock of whitewashing, low flying, smart-bombing seagulls was starting to leave.

Climbing, slipping, stumbling, balancing and sliding over tree roots was starting to wear a little thin, but it looked like another stretch of the same. There were also more boardwalks. I found the term "boardwalk" interesting – perhaps it was the image created by the song "Under the Boardwalk," which made me imagine summer holidays with white beaches, umbrellas, music, beach towels, squeals, laughter and the smell of Coppertone and hot dogs. Actually, I guess we had some of those things, but somehow the combination didn't create the same image as the song.

Boardwalks on the West Coast Trail are precisely that – a walk made by nailing cedar boards to tree trunks that are then laid across muddy areas in order to protect the environment. The fact that a hiker doesn't get as muddy is only a secondary benefit to protecting the undergrowth. The climate on Vancouver Island's west coast creates an incredible opportunity for plants and trees to flourish, but once they die, this same climate dramatically accelerates the deterioration and rot of these same plants and trees.

I can't quite make the connection between the human spirit and this highly activated life cycle of growth and death. This entire experience certainly quickens the heart rate and constantly allows time and space for regeneration. Maybe that's the only connection we need to make.

I'm not sure how many miles of boardwalk exist on the West Coast Trail, but they have increased significantly over the years. The wood surfaces we encountered were generally slick and often covered in moss, thus making an ideal roadway for a variety of snails and slugs that became our traveling companions. Many of the boards were broken or rotting through, and sometimes the whole assembly tipped and wobbled, forcing us to continue to maintain our focus on taking one step at a time. Missing boards also made it really easy to trip and fall in places.

A friend of mine had done that earlier in the year when she tripped on a boardwalk, and the weight of her backpack had propelled her forward to a perfect three-point landing. She just finished a hospital session with a plastic surgeon and I must say her nose looks great – again. I don't know if she has returned to finish the trail, but I'm sure there's a story in it.

For all the danger that lurked on these wooden paths, we made good time and kept a fairly steady pace. Many of the areas we traveled through had an other-worldly look and feel about them. The vegetation often differed from what we were used to. Some of the areas were quite open and bright, because they had very few trees. These boggy zones were full of lush lower growth and many flower species.

At the fun suspension bridge that crossed the Cheewhat River on that part of the trail, we put aside our "adult selves" and did what most kids do: jumped and danced and caused the whole structure to swing back and forth. I'm sure no one ever thought to do that before. Actually, I'm pretty sure I heard the echo of my mother's voice from long ago, something about, "Stop that Bobby, you'll fall and hurt yourself!" I still don't listen to my "inner mother."

In spite of cool and damp conditions, the exertions of carrying our packs, slogging up and down tree roots and climbing on and off boardwalks produced lots of body heat and sweat. A single layer of clothing was plenty to wear and soaking wet from perspiration in no time. When we did stop once in a while for a break, the moisture-filled air combined with the wet clothing to produce a pretty fast body chill. I was glad I was wearing a knit polyester top, because it wicked the moisture from my body and constantly made me want to disco dance. Who knew? The "Bee Gees" was short for Bob and Gord. In thinking back, I wonder whether, if we weren't careful, we could have contracted a case of "Saturday Night Fever?" Enough already – somebody stop me!

After the suspension bridge, it was a little less than two and a half miles to Nitinat Narrows, another crossroad on the trail that encouraged people to sit and share experiences. A wooden dock sat on the south side of the narrows, and as we approached we could hear laughter and discussions as various groups exchanged information about trail conditions ahead. Nitinat Narrows is like a funnel that connects Nitinat Lake to the Pacific Ocean. As the water from the lake joins the sea, it must rush through this narrow neck of a channel, creating very fast, deep water. It can't be crossed except by boat, and so once again a local family provided a ferry service to the other side.

Tables and chairs were conveniently set up on the dock so that travelers could enjoy a shore-side lunch, coincidentally for sale by our ferry pilot. Two days in a row, we were enjoying real food and, in fact, real good food. In this case, we were offered either barbecued salmon or fresh Dungeness crab. We eventually placed our orders for salmon and then settled down to enjoy a respite from the rigors of the trail.

It was amazing how cool we got from the breeze off the open water, and we both donned a sweater or jacket. We took advantage of the waiting time to once again check and adjust backpacks, and mostly talk with some of the people whom we knew and the ones who were coming from the other trail end. The same fellow who took the food orders also cooked the food and ran the boat back and forth across to the trailhead on the other side of the narrows. We couldn't see where the trail restarted, because it was around a bend, but it seemed that he was gone for about fifteen minutes to drop off and pick up more groups.

The menu consisted not just of food, but soft drinks and beer as well. Just like Chez Monique the day before, I was a little surprised at the number of people drinking beer, but I suppose that when I was younger I might have done the same. These days, or especially when I'm doing something physical like exercise or hiking, it seems counter-productive to drink beer or wine at the same time. I find as I get older that plain water has more appeal than ever. Seeing the beer cans on the tables brought about the reminder that we had been out of touch with the outside world for five days. This was heightened by the number of boats carrying sports fishermen to the mouth of the narrows. I do most of my fishing at the local supermarket in front of the coolers, but we were told by some of the fishermen that this was the premiere halibut fishing site on the West Coast. Later, when we crossed the inlet, we would see dozens of small watercraft jockeying for position in the dangerous currents and eddies.

We folks from the big city seem to assume that there is some sort of grand plan or an unseen organizational structure in place to coordinate the efforts of a busy place like this. I am always impressed when I witness people from rural or remote places who don't seem to get caught up in all that, but rather just do what's in front of them. I suspect that's a lot like living in the moment – and a subject of further writing in some future moment.

Our host at this outpost was busy preparing crab and salmon for diners, frequently jumping into his boat with a half-dozen or so hikers and heading out of sight to the trail and returning a few minutes later with another boatload of customers, or was that hikers? Somehow or other, during this activity, our orders got sidetracked and I'm glad they did. It's hard to get impatient and upset with someone who is obviously working very hard, especially in a setting as idyllic as Nitinat Narrows. We had time to explore our surroundings, and were fascinated by the process of preparing crabs for cooking.

The crabs were kept alive in a picnic cooler with holes drilled in it so water could enter, which was then dropped off the dock on the end of a rope. Whenever our cook/driver/tour guide received an order, he would pull the cooler up and take out the requested number of crabs, and then crack the crab on the dock surface and throw the waste pieces into the water. Like a cloud emerging from the depths of the inky water, thousands of salmon fingerlings would appear, feeding on the scraps and then disappearing to await the next treat. We watched this cycle of life unfold many times over the hour and a half lunch break.

Another side show put on for our benefit was the jellyfish production. In the shallows between the main dock and the shore, we spotted a jellyfish that would expand to the size and shape of a balloon and float through the shady water. Neither Gord nor I had ever seen one before, so this provided great entertainment. Once again, we city boys were wowed by something that was commonplace out here.

In a wooden shelter built at one end of the dock, where food and drinks were stored, we noticed some beautiful T-shirts hanging from the rafters. These commemorated the traveler's visit to Nitinat and had wonderful examples of First Nations art imprinted on them. We enjoyed looking at them, but decided that since we didn't want to add any weight at this juncture, we would probably purchase something like this at trail's end. Besides, it would have meant trying to locate our wallets inside our backpacks.

We had been waiting quite a while, but finally two plates of barbecued salmon and baked potatoes found their way to us and we dug in with enthusiasm. There is nothing like the taste of fresh salmon cooked over charcoal and served at dockside. The paper plate and plastic cutlery didn't matter as we dined alfresco and watched people arriving and departing. People-watching wasn't our only pastime; from our perch we could watch eagles soaring above the lake and over the trees. We learned later that one particular eagle made its permanent home here, which is very unusual since they are migratory birds.

We finished our lunch, repacked our gear and got ready to board the boat for the cruise over to the trailhead. There weren't many people at the narrows by then, except for some local fishermen, so somehow we had managed to spend almost two hours – during the day when we needed to cover the most distance – sitting and having lunch. We needed to make tracks to get to the campground.

The boat ride was short but enjoyable as we made our way across this beautiful expanse of water. On our right, green forest surrounded the lake, and on our left we could see the narrow opening that led to the Pacific Ocean. I'm not sure what the word Nitinat means in English, but it sure means a slice of heaven no matter how you say it.

I tried to drink in the sights and sounds of what I thought would be my last experience of Nitinat Narrows. I clearly remember thinking that I needed to enjoy the moment, because everything else – the daily stresses and problems – were just imagined, while this was real. We arrived at a small dock and the two of us jumped out of the boat, thanked our host and prepared to get moving again.

Speaking of movements, neither one of us had noticed a "natural decomposition chamber" back at the boat dock, but our map indicated that there was one on this side. We hitched up our backpacks, grabbed our hockey sticks and climbed up a steep pathway to find the trail and a badly needed environmentally responsible dumping station.

Taking turns using the facility allowed us to pass a number of fairly ribald comments back and forth while passing other things as well. Having unloaded, we reloaded our packs and headed up through the heavily forested trail. It was fairly slick and damp, and as usual we spent a lot of time climbing on and over roots, boulders and fallen trees. We felt under pressure because it was already well past 1 p.m. and we still had about five miles of trail to cover in order to make Tsusiat Falls, our planned and next available campsite. This was because we were traveling through First Nations-owned land, and no camping was allowed.

There is evidence of First Nations habitation in this area that dates back 6,500 years. Under any circumstances, a culture with that much history deserves our respect and admiration. They followed the cycles of the salmon and whale, migrating according to the availability of these food sources. Eventually, they established sizeable communities inland from the storm-ravaged shoreline, tending to follow various streams and rivers so that they could use their cedar dugouts for wide ranging transportation. Their claim to habitation and hunting rights predates the white settlers by more than 6,000 years. The entire West Coast Trail borders or crosses these traditional lands that the First Nations still depend on for survival, and they take great pride and a very active interest in protecting the resources of their territory. Without exception, we found the First Nations people we encountered to be helpful, friendly and happy, with a delightful sense of quiet humor.

We made our way through the trees well above the shoreline, catching only occasional glimpses of the surf hitting the rocks and beaches below. I was beginning to lag behind a bit, as the small footholds and constant slipping through the roots and mud began to get to me. I think I was also succumbing to a mild form of dehydration, as I only had the one water bottle and no hydration system in my backpack. The heavy workload and sweating depleted my reservoir of energy to the point that I was getting short-tempered and anxious to get out of the trees and on to the beach.

We would do this, but not before I heard Gord call from up ahead and tell me about a great viewpoint. I caught up to him and gazed down at a beautiful isolated cove, dotted with huge boulders that had broken away from the cliff and scattered onto the sand, with the high tide surf pounding into this scene with melodic rhythm. What a perfect setting and what a perfect opportunity to take a picture. A picture? That required a camera. Camera? Where the hell was my camera?

Gord checked his pockets and backpack, and I checked mine while experiencing the sinking feeling of knowing I had left it sitting on the table back at Nitinat Narrows an hour ago. I began to really feel the frustration. It's even possible that a discouraging word or two may have crossed my lips. This was, by far, the longest stretch of hiking we needed to do during the seven days and I was sorely tempted to forget the camera and forge ahead.

We talked about it briefly, though, and realized that would be a poor choice. It was the only operating camera we had, and it meant that we couldn't record anything on film in the days ahead. Not only was the camera back at Nitinat Narrows, but all the film we had shot so far was in the case with it. I suggested to Gord that he go ahead to the campsite while I retraced our steps and then headed to our campsite a little later. This seemed to me the best solution, since it was my camera and my mistake.

Sometimes in our journey, if we are lucky, we find people who will become friends for life. There are usually some key moments when these friendships are forged. This was another one, as Gord said no, that returning alone was not an option. He told me that we'd started this adventure together and if I wanted to go back for the camera – which he agreed with – then we would do that together, too! There was no false sense of integrity in his voice; he meant just what he said and sealed our friendship in that moment. There was no anger or resentment on his part – he simply decided that we would stick together and that was that.

With a sense of relief and gratitude, we adjusted our packs, turned around and headed back through the forest, through the roots and mud toward the dock where we had been dropped off so recently. We both began wondering how often the ferry service ran, and consequently how long we might have to wait for a ride across Nitinat Narrows. We were also very concerned about having enough time to cross the narrows, get the camera, retrace our steps and then press on to the campsite. This was the one day when we had no alternative campsites available to spend the night at.

We moved as quickly as we could, the sense of urgency creating more energy in our strides. As we got closer to the north side of Nitinat, we could hear voices and so we quickened our pace, climbed down to the water level and came upon three people with their own boat. It turned out to be a father, son and grandfather who had tied up at the dock to organize their fishing gear before heading out into the channel. Introductions made all around, we shared our predicament about the camera and asked if they had seen the ferry recently. The boat owner would hear none of that as he offered to take us across the channel and back in his boat.

The older I get, the more I find the world full of selfless, caring and willing people like that. There wasn't a moment's hesitation as this gentleman offered his assistance. It happened that these three men had come in from the east side of Vancouver Island to do some intergenerational fishing and enjoy each other's company.

It's a small world and as we chatted, we discovered some mutual acquaintances and also discovered that the boat owner was the brother of a prominent member of parliament from our home town of Calgary – thus making the older man her father. They didn't check our political affiliation before offering us the ride either. They probably still don't realize that we both were politically aligned with the philosophy of that same MP.

While we talked, Gord could see that the oldest fellow was having difficulty putting together a herring jig to get ready for their fishing excursion, so he stepped up and offered his assistance. Now we felt an even trade had been brokered – I would get a ride across to pick up my camera while Gord put together their fishing tackle. I always feel better when people's generosity can be repaid, even if it was Gord doing the repaying.

I stepped down into the boat and the young lad pushed us away from the dock. We headed out across the channel and about three quarters of the way across encountered the ferry coming toward us. A quick wave and both craft slowed so the ferry pilot could tell me where my camera was and wish us good luck. We continued on to the site of our lunch break. I hopped on to the dock and into the storage area, retrieved my camera and case, and jumped back into the boat in a couple of minutes.

My rescuer was a talkative guy and we soon discovered some common acquaintances in the investment industry in Vancouver where he worked. I had been involved in that industry many years earlier when I worked for a Vancouver-based brokerage house in their Winnipeg office. I didn't offer too many opinions about the various characters we discussed – that too could be the subject of some future writing!

As we approached the dock on the north side of the narrows for the second time that day, the ferry was setting out for its return journey. I shouted my thanks as I waved my camera, feeling an enormous sense of relief that we could get underway happily.

We tied up at the dock. Gord had completed refitting the fishing gear, so our two groups wished each other luck and thanks as Gord and I once again headed up the trail. Urgency, heightened with a touch of anxiety, began to drive us forward. It was early afternoon and we were usually setting up camp by this time. We had more than four miles to go.

I've mentioned this before, but it really amazes me in retrospect how we allowed time to rule our feelings. We probably had seven hours of daylight, and we knew we wouldn't have to sleep hanging from a tree branch – there was always lots of beach to camp on. We realize now that the only real danger we faced was from the stress within ourselves.

But, not knowing that, we plunged on toward our next "moment," back over the same tree roots and muddy pathways

– familiarity not making it any easier. I could feel my own intensity level rising with each slip, slide and step. This drudgery went on for almost two miles, and thanks to the camera episode, I was reaching my limit when we came upon another beach access point. I needed a change of scenery and I suggested we move onto the beach and take a break. The trail was already at water level at this point, so there were no ladders or cliffs; we simply walked out onto the beach, found some logs and lowered our packs onto them.

I sensed Gord's frustration with my need for rest and could tell that he was anxious to saddle up and get back on the trail. He was tired too. We looked at the map and realized that we could either return to the trail through the forest or walk in the sand on the beach for at least the next mile or so. Now we get back to foot size determining the route that was best for us. We had two totally different perspectives about the route/root to take.

The day was still overcast and misty, and we could clearly see many boot tracks in the sand heading in both directions. I made up my mind. I no longer cared how difficult walking on the sand was for Gord – I just knew that I wasn't going to walk over those roots again today, and that was that. I told Gord that I didn't give a damn what he decided, but I was walking on the beach and he could do whatever the hell he wanted!

With that, I turned around and started walking north on the beach, trying to stick with the hard-packed sand wherever possible. Gord didn't have his backpack on yet and I simply left him to stare after me. A year later, we still laugh about this incident, but in that moment, neither of us was laughing. We were both feeling the anxiety, frustration and anger generated by the lack of water and the level of physical exhaustion that creeps up after four days and nights of constant duress. Add four days and nights of constant companionship and the little things start to take on larger proportions. It's not a lot different from a marriage – those little habits that we found humorous earlier had graduated beyond eccentric to the focal point of petty anger. This marriage of convenience was breaking up on the rocky shoals – I knew because I was walking on them.

I was also walking with that stiff back, stiff legs, arms swinging, stare straight ahead, teeth clenched determination that comes from knowing "I'm right – he's wrong!" Gord has a nice picture, snapped with my camera, of my "best side" disappearing into the mist about two hundred yards down the beach. I eventually turned around to see whether he was following me up the beach or had returned to the forest trail. I was relieved to see that he began what was a grueling trek through the sand behind me.

This forced walk on my part eventually took some of the starch out of my "rightness," and realizing that my partner had forsaken the route that was easier for him added a little guilt to my cauldron of emotions. I was thinking that a nice meal of humble soup would be coming up soon. Even though my size thirteen boots acted like snowshoes as I walked over the sand, it still took an enormous amount of energy to carry forty-five pounds on my back and use brute strength, step after step, for more than a mile. I continued to tire and slow down – so Gord could catch up – but up ahead was something I simply didn't anticipate.

We had seen a picture of this somewhere, but didn't realize that this was the stretch of beach where the Hole in the Wall was located. It's not mentioned on the Parks Canada map, although it's in most of the guidebooks – none of which we had consulted that day. The map did, however, inform us that this particular section at Tsusiat Point was only passable at tides below nine feet, and neither of us had any real clue where we were in terms of the tide table. Sometimes it's better to have good luck than good organization, or in my case, good manners. If I hadn't stomped ahead and insisted upon walking the beach, we might not have seen this major attraction of the trail. This highlights the importance of using a good reference guide, and there are many available – just not in our backpacks.

We didn't really say too much at that time about our earlier tiff, but realized that we would just be able to make it through that unique geological feature before the tide came in and blocked our route along the rest of the beach. That would have meant retracing our steps yet again, and was not something either of us was prepared to contemplate. We hurriedly took a few pictures of each other going through the hole and gingerly made our way over the rocks that were still accessible to the beach on the north side.

It was late afternoon and we began to realize that we didn't need to panic with regard to time – we had lots – a little less than a mile and a quarter to go. We were too tired to push very hard, but tried to keep the pace by putting one foot in front of the other – one step at a time.

I felt some sort of vindication for my earlier behavior because without it, we wouldn't have seen the Hole in the Wall, but we were both too tired to really discuss it at length. We were now focused on getting to Tsusiat Falls and grinding our way through the sand with what strength we had left. For most of our hike on the West Coast Trail, Gord would walk out in front and lead the way. We joked that this was because I'm taller and if I was in front, he would have trouble enjoying the view ahead.

The two truths about this are that no one can really enjoy the view ahead, as you are forced to totally concentrate on your next footstep – especially in the forest. And secondly, I simply walk at a slower pace than Gord. The few times that I took the lead, he was walking right on my heels, so it was just easier for both of us if Gord led. On the sand, however, the roles reversed and we settled into our own speed and rhythm. Every once in a while, the guy in front would stop so the other could catch up and generally we would take a drink of water and a snack. Sometimes we would remove our backpacks and have a longer rest break, but often, as on that day, we would simply stop for a few minutes and then head out again.

We knew we were coming to the end of a very long day, but the end wasn't coming fast enough. All we could see ahead of us was more sand. At the foot of a rise, I waited for Gord to catch up. I really just needed more rest, because I was pretty close to finished.

He didn't look much better and we were both so exhausted that neither of us felt much like sharing words: the looks and thoughts that passed between us spoke volumes about how tired we were.

Maybe we could catch a glimpse of our goal from the top of this next sand mogul – if we could get up it. Very slowly and laboriously we made our way up the little sand dune, realizing as we got close to the top that we had finally made it. In the distance we could see Tsusiat Falls and the pool of water at its base. Between us and the falls, all sorts of logs and tents stretched out in the sand. We just needed to find a reasonably flat site for our tent, set it up, filter fresh water, make dinner, organize our stuff, set up a tarp, unload sleeping mats and bags, and generally relax and enjoy one of the most picturesque and popular campsites on the trail.

It was so tempting to peel off my clothes and jump into that pool of water, but I was feeling rather contrite and knew that my partner would want to get all of our chores done first, so we began scouting a location.

Even though we had arrived many hours later than usual, and this was obviously the busiest campsite we had encountered so far, we had very little trouble securing a spot among the logs. The site was relatively level and we were even able to wedge a couple of poles into a stack of logs in such a way that we could stretch a tarp overtop and create a great cooking shelter. We were about a hundred yards from the waterfall and dangerously out of drinking water, so Gord headed for the freshwater pool while I set up the tent.

The cool temperatures were keeping most people out of the water and it wasn't long before I lost the desire to peel off clothes and go for a dip. In fact, I found my fleece and put it on in relatively short order. Some brave souls were going in the water to clean up, but they didn't stay in long – something about shrinkage. No one sat under the waterfalls as they'd done in some of the videos, but this was still an absolutely beautiful spot that represented all that was worthwhile about hiking the West Coast Trail.

Apparently other people agreed, as there were probably fifty tents set up, easily double the number we had seen anywhere else. We learned that many people made this a two-day stop and who could blame them? Lots of fresh water, a big wide beach with a waterfall in the middle, ocean-front campsites – Tsusiat is worth the price of admission all by itself.

Gord returned with full water bottles and we quickly got some water on to boil for tea. Replacing the fluid levels made a big difference in how we functioned physically and mentally, not just on that day, but every day. It wasn't long before we had dinner cooking over the now familiar one-burner stove, and some semblance of order and normalcy was returning to our existence. We both talked about and apologized for the incident earlier on the beach and let it go very easily. We still have a good chuckle when reminding each other about it on various occasions. Our objective is to embarrass the other person – too bad we're both playing the same game and that it doesn't work. Oh well, the minds of little boys at play.

We learned that the fire ban had finally been lifted, but I think we were too tired to bother building a campfire of our own. Besides, that would mean that somebody had to stay up to make sure it was out. We knew we would be "out" long before that, as dark was approaching along with the Sandman.

The young fellow that had helped us a few nights earlier with our water filter and then later with hanging the food bags, was camped right next to us with his wife. They were pretty experienced campers and had left their kids at home while they hiked the West Coast Trail. In contrast to Gord and me, they had obviously spent a lot of time researching the trail and had taken hundreds of photos along the journey. They were also using a different trail guide, which was much better at describing the various campsites and routes.

Their attitude was friendly and open, and – like so many others – they were willing and eager to discuss their adventure. Gord and I quickly accepted their invitation to join them around the fire. It was beginning to feel pretty chilly with the dampness penetrating our clothes as dusk descended. The heat from the flames, combined with a cup of hot tea, warmed the body and soul, as did the conversation about families, the trail, whales and equipment.

Gord and our friend compared features of headlamps and I heard words like candlepower, LED and halogen – all very interesting. His wife began talking about the growing legend of "the hockey stick hikers," as our story seemed to be spreading even further. She made us promise to wake them in the morning before we left so they could take pictures. So there's now photographic evidence in somebody's scrapbook of our trek and our hockey sticks. It was about this time that we began referring to ourselves as the hockey stick hikers.

As I look back on it, it's funny how testosterone comes into play when men reach middle age. Gord and I were quite careful to bring up the subject of wives and children when talking with other hikers. It's humorous when I think about the fact that we were defending our position as friends as opposed to "special friends." We were always pretty conscious of this as we turned in at nightfall, thinking we had to justify being tired and getting into the same tent – like who cared?

After a nice conversation and the warmth of the tea and fire, we took our manly selves to our tent and called it a night. There was a certain contentedness as we lay in our sleeping bags discussing the events of the day and solving some of life's puzzles. We had survived the "Day Five Fight" and remained friends, covered about ten miles of trail and generally felt pretty satisfied with having made it this far without injury to body or soul.

Our friends had decided to stay at Tsusiat Falls for another day to rest and relax. They were truly enjoying every moment of this experience, and I thought what a great trait to pass on to their children – to live in and enjoy the moment.

In the city, some kinds of noise become white noise as we learn to accept the sounds of cars, televisions, talking, machinery, etc. into our consciousness and no longer hear them. While I got used to the sounds of the waves, even the powerful pounding of the crashing surf, they didn't really become white noise but rather a rhythmic life force that offered a sense of place and position. When I kept the sound of the waves on my left, I knew I was heading north. Knowing where the water was, especially in the pitch black of night, seemed like a good idea when I awoke to find "relief." There could be some kind of metaphor developing here, but I decided to sleep on it first.

# Day Six

A pretty typical morning for us on the trail – overcast, a little drizzle, the tent wet – but fortunately the tarp we had rigged the night before had kept our backpacks and other gear dry.

We were gradually getting away from the idea of having to hurry to get to the next campsite, and so we started the stove, got some water boiling and made oatmeal and coffee. This also gave the tent fly some extra time in the breeze to dry and, more importantly, allowed us to take on some nutrition and liquid. We were finally getting reasonably adept at packing our belongings and adjusting our packs – just in time for us to head toward our last night on the trail, although that hadn't really hit home for us yet.

Our friends from the previous night were up and about too, so after eating breakfast and filtering fresh water, we packed up and posed for some pictures. Their extra day here at Tsusiat Falls meant that we wouldn't see them again. We said our goodbyes and thank yous for the help, made sure the rain covers on our packs were tight, and set out to regain the trail.

We had passed the trail access the day before, so we retraced our steps in the sand and began to ascend some pretty formidable ladders, up to the forest and its pathway. After the ladders, the trail was rather civilized by WCT standards, and it wasn't long before we had trooped the mile or so through the rainforest to the Klanawa River. Up until that point, we hadn't needed to employ the cable cars to cross the various creeks and rivers, because the water was always low enough to wade through using nature's stepping stones. This resulted in the odd bit of water in our boots, but by now that was a good thing!

The river before us, however, was wide, fast and deep – kind of like my high school love life. (I don't know where that came from but if any of the young ladies involved are reading this, please understand that you represent the "deep" part of my life. Whew!) The only way to cross the Klanawa River was by using the handy cable car provided by Parks Canada. Now don't misunderstand, this was not San Francisco – there were no Rice-a-Roni commercials being shot and Tony Bennett would really leave his heart here if he tried to hike the WCT at his age. The cable cars were steel buckets with two wheels on top hanging from a thick steel cable suspended between two towers on either side of the river. There was almost enough room for two old guys and their packs – oops, almost forgot the hockey sticks.

We wedged ourselves into the car as best we could and tried to push ourselves off the platform and out into the void. It was easier when I lifted my fat butt up off the seat and took the extra strain off the cables so that the car could move. The first part was fun in a Disney ride kind of way, as you free fall down the sagging cable to the midpoint of the river. This was followed by a hand-over-hand pulling of the car filled with backpacks and two round little bellies up the other side to the platform. Naturally, as we were struggling with this, another group of hikers (much younger) showed up on the platform we had just abandoned to view our efforts and wait patiently for the car to return. Before we could send it back to them, we had to pry ourselves and equipment from this sardine can – a work of form and beauty if there ever was one.

We descended more ladders down off the platform and then on to reclaim the trail itself. We had some small degree of difficulty here in following the trail, but of the WCT's forty-seven miles, this was the only spot where this occurred and it was just a minor misdirection that I'll blame on Gord – he can write his own book! We made our way to the mouth of the river and the beach after admiring what I thought were cougar tracks in the soft mud. If there was one around, I'm sure it would be more discerning than to bother two tough old birds that smelled like us. We never did see a cougar the whole length of the trail, unfortunately.

We found ourselves back on the beach and took a quick break to enjoy the emerging sunshine and the fabulous ocean view from a convenient log. Then we were marching through the sand again and across the rock shelf, beginning to realize this was developing into a pretty terrific day. We were starting to get the hang of this walking thing: trail hardened and in much better physical condition than when we'd started, we'd lightened our loads and our spirits, as well. At that moment, walking along the shoreline of the West Coast Trail – especially after the anxiety of not knowing if we would be able to do it – was an experience on so many levels, like none other. It was, truly, a great moment to be alive.

We hiked on through this idyll for the rest of the morning, drinking in the sights, sounds and smells while keeping an eye on the ocean for signs of whales. We both really wanted to see some, but knew that this wasn't the high season for whale watching. A few generally stay around for a larger portion of the year, though, and so we hoped to have the opportunity to watch them.

A quick map check showed us that we would soon have to move back into the forest, since we were approaching another impassable surge channel. The instructions showed an anchor from a shipwreck lying on the rocks near the beach access point. I began watching carefully for the anchor, without success.

I knew we were close to it but – even with my binoculars – I couldn't see it no matter how hard I looked. We reached the surge channel, which looked like a good spot to relax and have something to eat since it was about noon anyway. We found a nice big log and dumped our packs and settled in for a leisurely lunch. Another party of hikers had chosen a small cove behind us and was taking in the sunshine and some food, as well.

We were thoroughly enjoying the brief reverie when we spotted two young men, traveling very light, coming toward us from the north. No big backpacks, and it appeared one of them was actually wearing sandals. These two were climbing over and through the cliff face that had some pretty rugged rock formations and steep drop-offs. As they climbed down near us, we could see that they were wearing uniform shirts, so we assumed that we were about to get a parking ticket. (I really do have to do something about that oversized trailer I'm dragging around behind me.) They asked if they could join us on the log while they ate their lunch. We said, "of course," and realized that they were part of the First Nations guardian force that patrolled the trail to ensure the safety of the hikers and the environment alike.

Instantly likeable, they each pulled a sandwich out of their pocket and asked how our hike was going. Their nature was to be fairly quiet, but what wonderful ambassadors for the people whose land the WCT borders. Their love for this part of the world was so noticeable and refreshing in people so young. Gord and I thoroughly enjoyed their company for lunch. One of them was carrying a wooden walking stick, instantly making him an honorary "hockey stick hiker."

I asked him about the decoration on the top end of the bare alder wood staff. He shared the fact that his father was concerned about the presence of a cougar in the vicinity, and had carved it as a form of protection while his son patrolled his assigned area of the trail. He showed us the carved head of a killer whale that then transformed into the head of a wolf on the tip of the shaft. According to legend, when the killer whale moves on to land it becomes a wolf and would protect him from the cougar – which also helped to explain why the killer whale is often referred to as the sea wolf.

For me, it was also a beautiful story that illustrated the love of a father for a son and the deeply felt spirituality of a gentle people. Gord and I are both bent a little in the direction of spirituality, and this served as the perfect example for us of the link between the First Nations culture and God or the spirit reflected in the earth.

We were kind of expecting this trip to have some sort of spiritual effect on us and, looking back, this was the ideal demonstration of our own long-held beliefs. We have much to learn from nature, the earth, the sea and the people most closely connected to them. And when we find this link, it is impossible to knowingly despoil an area as beautiful as this by introducing any sort of polluting products that could create permanent damage.

Speaking of manmade objects, I asked our hosts (because that was what they were) about the anchor that was noted on the map. I showed them how it indicated that the shipwrecked item was supposed to be very near us, but I couldn't see it no matter how carefully I surveyed the beach before me. The older of the two looked at me, then inclined his head to the right and said, "You mean that anchor there?" About twenty feet behind us, between the log and the cliff face, sat a huge rusting anchor, just like the map showed.

These two young men had far too much class to let their heads drop back, roll their eyes and exclaim "City People!" Their amusement shone brightly on their faces, however, as they wished us good luck and got underway again. A year later, and Gord is still laughing at me over that one. The guys took a picture of us sitting on the log, enjoying the sunshine, which still hangs in my kitchen at home. For me, those few moments captured the true spirit of the West Coast Trail.

We were at mile twelve and still had five to go in order to reach our planned campsite for the night at Michigan Creek. We climbed back up the cliff face from the beach using some ropes and salal bushes for purchase. Once we regained the trail, we continued climbing through undergrowth toward the Valencia Bluffs, which were named after the ship that went down in 1906 with the loss of 133 lives. (Almost 134, but don't tell Gord's wife, because she would only worry.)

The path was relatively narrow and, in spots, came within inches of the cliff edge, where the ground dropped sharply away some one to two hundred feet to the rocks and waves below. We availed ourselves of an abundance of lookouts and picture-taking opportunities.

Tree roots still crossed the path here and there, so we had to move with some caution, but generally this was a pleasant part of the hike. Did I say we had to be careful? Frankly, we needed to be vigilant, because in places, a misstep could have sent us tumbling down to our maker – or whoever awaited us below on the rocks.

Gord was out in front, as usual, and I wasn't watching him and he doesn't really remember how, but he stumbled. The weight of his pack propelled him forward off the trail and toward the cliff. I heard him yell, heard a thud, and by the time I got there he was plastered against a tree. Somehow, he had twisted around as he fell and his backpack took the brunt of the collision. Good thing: a few more feet and the results could have been a lot different. He was obviously dazed, but didn't need my help as I rushed over and stretched out my hockey stick for him to grab and pull himself back on to the trail.

He had narrowly missed the fall into oblivion and needed a few moments to get his breath and check for damage. Incidents like this were probably the very things our wives at home were worrying about. Oh well: it creates character, sometimes known as gray hair, and results in stories to tell the grandchildren. Never underestimate the importance of those stories – like the time when I was a kid playing hockey on the lake and had that breakaway...wove my way through the opposing players...skated the length of two hockey rinks...wound up for the supersonic slapshot on goal...and won the Stanley Cup. Ahem!

We sorted ourselves out, took a short break and resumed our trek, albeit a little more cautiously. Our reward was finding a fabulous lookout with a high bench built beside the trail – a great spot to rest a backpack, enjoy the surf pounding the shore below, and remove the enormous boulder I'd found in my boot.

We passed Tsocowis Creek and returned to the beach to finish our walk to Michigan Creek about three miles farther on. It was mid-afternoon, the sun was shining and a certain arrogance had settled into our gait. We knew we were nearing the end, that this would be our last night and that we were meeting people coming from the other end who were only on their second day of hiking. They were easy to spot, with their clean clothes and enthusiastic eyes – rookies! There seemed to be a silent code among the hikers who were finishing the trail to keep the difficulty level to themselves. We didn't want to wreck the fun for those who thought that what they had completed so far was representative of what lay ahead.

It's a little bit like being in a building supply store on a Saturday afternoon, watching the male of the species strut his stuff. It was the same here, as the guys took the lead: you could overhear them telling their girlfriends or wives all the ins and outs of backpacking the WCT. Those of us coming from the Port Renfrew end occasionally caught snatches of conversation about how difficult these people had had it so far, but held firm to our unspoken knowing. We probably had some right to the arrogance that had crept in with the knowledge that we had almost accomplished something very special. It's a small and select group of people who have completed the West Coast Trail.

We arrived at the Michigan Creek campsite in late afternoon and decided on a spot near the trees, overlooking a shelf where some gray whales were apparently feeding. Finally, whales to watch, but first we would pitch our tent in the sand. The beach sloped down from the cliff behind us in the spot we chose, so we found a piece of flat driftwood about five feet long and began to prepare a level surface. We grabbed opposite ends of the board and used it like the blade on a road grader to move sand from the cliff side toward the water and create a pool table-like platform to place our tent for the final night.

A few minutes spent doing this and we had to stand back and admire our construction skills and wonder why we hadn't made careers out of managing huge earthmoving projects – what a thing of beauty and symmetry. Anyone need a dam built? With the tent pitched, sleeping bags and pads thrown inside, our backpacks emptied out and cooking utensils, stove, etc. laid out for the evening banquet, we walked toward the ocean to watch the whale show apparently scheduled for 4 p.m.

There were four or five people out on the edge of the rock shelf, some with large cameras, enjoying and photographing these enormous gray whales as they fed. What a magnificent sight to watch these creatures breaching and blowing so close to us. Besides, the admission price was so much lower than SeaWorld, although we had to make do without the bikini-clad attendants throwing fish. (Sorry, spending six or seven nights in a tent with another guy can cause your mind to wander.) We enjoyed a front row center seat for the fishing demonstration, which appeared to be a long-term feature, so after about twenty minutes we returned to our tent site, filtered some water and began preparing our own dinner while keeping an eye on the whales through the binoculars.

Watching the whales eat inspired me to open the foil pack of tuna and add it to the night's entrée of fairly plain pasta. I enjoyed it, as I did most of the meals, but Gord had soup and passed on the epicurean delight. The campsite was not particularly crowded on that night, but we took notice of two guys who had set up near us.

They were formidable in appearance and we got the impression that they may have left their "hogs" at the trailhead, ditched their leathers and decided to conquer the West Coast Trail. Gord and I both noticed our "Spidey senses" tingling as these two very gregarious woodsmen began to loudly stake their claim. It was their first night, so their boisterous nature could be excused, but we noticed a rather odd assortment of gear compared to everyone else. The WCT is a pretty intense backpacking test, and equipment weight tends to be everyone's primary concern – for good reason. In most cases, anything that is bulky, heavy or a luxury is jettisoned long before starting the hike. What caught our attention was the cast iron cooking pot, oversized canvas tent and lantern – things that no one brings on this trek.

I'm sure it was just our overactive imaginations, but Gord and I began to create a story to explain these two. In our minds, they acted the part of escaped prisoners on the lam, intending to hide out on the Pacific Coast. Visions of "Deliverance" danced in our heads as we speculated that their fairly aggressive approaches to some of the women in the campground indicated a lengthy stay in the Gray Bar Hotel. I am absolutely positive that this whole story was the product of our over active imaginations and maybe reflects our forced abstinence from television.

In any case, we kept our distance and had very little to do with them, although when we were filtering water at a small pool, one of them provided entertainment in the form of nude bathing. This greatly influenced both the speed of filtering and the placement of our intake tube. Not a pretty picture, but then again, I'm sure we weren't either – at least, I know Gord wasn't after seven days in the wilderness. I'd conveniently left the mirror behind, but I'm sure my matinee idol appearance was still intact.

After dinner and cleaning up, I sat on a log with a cup of tea and noticed in the southwest sky, just above the horizon, a plane coming toward us. Its bright white nose light was directly in my line of sight, but it was a few minutes before I realized that it wasn't actually moving. I assumed it was coming straight toward us, which would account for its intensity, with the onset of dusk explaining my inability to see the plane's fuselage. But it didn't turn, didn't get any bigger and just seemed to sit there in the sky.

It was one of our few clear nights, and I wondered if this was just a particularly bright star. Then it occurred to me that stars twinkle and this light was just staring at me like a white, unblinking eye. No, it wasn't a UFO…it had to be a planet. That's when I remembered reading in the Calgary Herald before we left to hike the trail that Mars, on this specific day, was closer to Earth than at any time in the previous 65,000 years. (I have no idea how they figure that stuff out.)

Word of this unique phenomenon spread from group to group and everyone began to exchange thoughts on the significance of this sighting. It added an exclamation point to the night and the entire experience for me. I don't know that this has any particular social, historical or spiritual meaning, but it was just such a great way to experience something that seemed to demonstrate our own place and importance in the universe.

Our last night on the trail took on a special significance for us. We began sharing the various things that had occurred over the past week. In some ways it seemed much longer than six days, and in other ways, shorter. In all ways, we both began to realize the changes we were making physically and emotionally. We knew that we had accomplished something very important in both of our lives. It would be interesting to see what the results would be in the days, months and years ahead. No question that we were both in the best physical condition we had been in many years.

A group of four women arrived and set up camp in front of us, clearly having a ball. They were hiking the trail from the same end we had started at, but were completing it in five days instead of seven. It was great to see the energy and joy they expressed as they set up tents, cooked dinner and rebuffed the advances of our two erstwhile jail breakers. We never really figured out the exact relationship, but this foursome was probably two mothers and daughters who were obviously very athletic and totally enjoying each other's company and the experience they were sharing. I think it's the same story for most people on this adventure. The West Coast Trail combines the kinds of challenges, frustrations, victories and raw beauty that make this the experience of a lifetime for most hikers. Watching other people show this energy brought validity to our own feelings, and created a lifetime bond with anyone else who has had the experience.

The campground traffic was slowing down as dark descended and people gradually made their way to their tents, some anticipating several tomorrows on the trail and many, like us, contemplating the final push to the end. We hadn't spent any time inside our tent since we set it up, but – before turning in – we had to arrange sleeping pads, bags and pillows. That's when we noticed the sensation of crawling uphill to access the sleeping bag openings. We began to wonder about our site clearing skills or, at least, our ability to create a level sleeping field. It was too dark, we were too tired and it was too late to bother doing anything about it.

We turned in and settled down for a night's sleep. We had earned it as we reviewed the day's happenings and enjoyed the aroma of ripe boots and underwear.

## DAY SEVEN

I had the sensation of riding down a waterslide during my sleep. I don't know what Freud would say about that – there may be some connection between the Id and the Ego – but it probably had more to do with our earth-moving skills from the previous day.

Since the ground sloped from our head down to our feet, and since sleeping bags are often slippery affairs, I found myself struggling to stay in one place and Gord appeared to have forgotten the Velcro. It turned out to be an exciting night as we created the video for the song "Slip, slidin' away." I found myself folded up in the bottom half of my sleeping bag a couple of times. Good thing the tent had a strong zipper on it, or I might have ended up sleeping on the sand in front of it. Oh well: it's all good, and contributes to the memories.

We'd been so proud of our site-leveling acumen, but perhaps it wasn't ready for world-scale projects just yet. I guess we hadn't done too great a job of smoothing out the tent site. It had looked good from my angle – like my picture hanging at home – but apparently, I see life "off kilter" a bit. (Many family and friends would agree with that statement!)

After a few laughs, we crawled out of the tent and made some oatmeal for breakfast and started cleaning up and repacking our equipment for the last time. We had about seven and a half miles to cover to the trail's end, where we had to find transportation to Bamfield and then to Port Renfrew to pick up the car and drive down to Victoria. We had a full day ahead of us, even though everyone told us that this end of the trek was the easiest. In any case, we headed back up to the trail from Michigan Creek. Others were breaking camp as well, and we stood for a few moments of nostalgia to admire the view, knowing that we would be hiking through forest for the day and wouldn't be at water's edge again.

A little less than a mile down the trail, we found the Pachena Lighthouse. Despite our steady pace, the trail wasn't totally without challenge here. The elevation increased continually from Michigan to the lighthouse, although nothing we couldn't handle. The ever-present roots, however, continued to remind us that we still couldn't lose our focus on the step ahead. We didn't completely lose the constantly changing face of the Pacific Ocean, thanks to several viewpoints along the way, but with roots, mud and logs it was still "one step at a time."

A quick look at the view from Pachena Lighthouse and we were on our way again, becoming more aware of the clock – re-entering civilization seems to require attention to hours and minutes rather than the natural rhythms found in the wilderness. The trail along that section was still pretty narrow and with the twists and turns, you couldn't see all that far ahead. Foot traffic coming toward us started to gather steam as first-day hikers were coming from the trailhead and local First Nations people were hiking into their villages with supplies. It wasn't uncommon to be surprised by a couple of hikers on the other side of a tree as the trail twisted its way through the forest. Sometimes other surprises showed up as well.

As always, Gord was well out in front, breaking trail, and beyond my sight. We were in fairly narrow quarters as the brush on either side threatened to reclaim the path. Gord turned a corner and a four-legged monster, black and shiny with a head the size of, well the size of a bear, came bounding toward him.

I can only imagine the lump in his throat as his biggest fear materialized before his eyes. It's a case of when a second seems like an hour, but in that fear-stretched moment, the bear of his mind became a dog of the flesh. (Perhaps the wagging tail held a clue to its identity and intentions.)

We hadn't seen any domesticated animals since we started, except at Chez Monique, because hikers aren't allowed to take them on the trail, so this unexpected visitor caused one of those "holy shit" moments for my partner. By the time I came upon them, all was well and the First Nations family who belonged to the big black Rottweiler came along the path carrying heavy loads of provisions and chuckling at our expense. Calm was restored and I'm sure

Gord's heart beat eventually returned to normal as we continued on our adventure, anticipating a quiet finish on the still fairly strenuous path.

As we reached a fairly mucky, low-lying area with some split logs laid down to provide footing, we met a group of four men and a boy heading south. As always, especially on that last day, we all stopped to talk and trade information on trail conditions, hazards and difficulties. The young lad spotted our hockey sticks and found this quite novel as they were all sporting name-brand hiking poles. It turned out that this pre-teen was hiking with his dad, uncle and both grandfathers. Some discussion ensued about our use of hockey sticks for support, and one of the grandfathers must have thought we were somehow connected in hockey circles. He took great pride in informing us about the virtues of his freckle-faced, red-haired grandson as a highly sought-after goaltender in the B.C. Interior.

I've spent enough time over the years with my nose pressed to the glass around a hockey rink to recognize the promotion. To excel in any sport requires more than just skill, strength and desire – it requires opportunity. Opportunity often comes from unlikely sources, and I think Grandpa was simply making use of this opportunity just in case the two guys with hockey sticks could help his grandson. Not only have I witnessed this behavior before, I know I have engaged in the same thing myself on occasion. (So, if you're reading this, Grandpa – good on you! Sorry I couldn't help.) As always, we wished each other good luck, and headed in opposite directions.

In some ways, these final few miles of trail were a little like the first few, in their quiet majesty: towering trees, stillness, earthy smells, damp, dense, green – magnificent. The terrain was, however, not nearly as physically demanding, and I was doing some mental arithmetic that indicated our speed was two and a half miles per hour, compared to Day One when our speed was two-thirds of a mile per hour – a big difference! At this rate, I calculated, we would be at the trailhead around 11 a.m. That meant the possibility of lunch in civilization!

Most hiking books recommend that trekkers stay together and that the pace of a group should be the same as its slowest member. That would be me. On Day Two, I got into some trouble on the rocks and as the last member of our small troop, there was no immediate help available. The same thing can happen to the hiker who is in the lead and out of sight of the rest of the entourage. The proof of the wisdom about sticking close together was coming closer, but first we were going to enjoy the only part of this experience that fits my description of a trail.

I don't know what image your mind conjures up when you hear the word "trail." I suppose it's based on previous experience, but somehow, in my utopia, I'd imagined a pathway about six feet wide, covered in gravel, fairly flat and winding its way through the trees. I'm surprised I didn't include music from the "Wizard of Oz" as I reread this description.

Well, we encountered our "Yellow Brick Road" at about this point in the adventure. Indeed, there is a stretch, and we took pictures to prove it, where we could walk side by side, enjoying the sights, smells and sounds while munching on trail mix, all at the same time. For the only time during those seven days, we didn't have to stop and consciously choose where to place our boot to make a safe next step.

When I look back on it, I think it was this particular stretch that I had trained for back home, walking in Fish Creek Park. This piece of paradise lasted exactly fifteen minutes or two-thirds of a mile by my reckoning, and then the roots returned. At this point, we had about an hour to go to reach the end of the road, and I think we were both concentrating on drinking in every last drop of the experience. Sure, we were tired, hungry and thirsty, but it was very apparent to us both that this had been a very special week in our lives. Absorbing the sensory banquet probably took some of the focus out of our meandering as we came back into twisting forest routes with dense vegetation on both sides.

We were hiking in single file again, closer together than normal, maybe twenty-five feet apart. I was enjoying the view of the back of Gord's backpack and he was, as usual, on the lookout for interesting sights – as much as someone who should wear glasses, but doesn't, can be on the lookout. He assumes that I saw the same thing he did and until he reads this, won't realize that I didn't witness any part of this real-life moment. I can only record what he reported to me after I heard him yell with obvious fear in his voice.

During one of our training hikes in Kananaskis Country, Gord spied a head peeking out of the woods and tried to alert me. I heard him almost complete the word "Puma." Somehow, his mind wanted to say Puma instead of "Cougar!" There was no mistake this time, however, as he yelled "Bear!"

I don't make fun of Gord's fear of bears. I understand completely, as I have the same fear of snakes. My wife has a similar, uncontrollable horror of moths that always results in panic, screaming, running, confusion and chaos. So, sometimes I may make a remark or two about that and it may sound less than complimentary. She may rewrite this line as she types my manuscript but take it from me: I mention this in only the most supportive way.

Back to Gord, who was on the trail and facing an uncertain future. Just an hour or so earlier, his heart had pumped through his throat at the sight of the huge black dog that had suddenly appeared before him. Kind of like a Hitchcock movie, just when the adrenaline comes back to normal and the music is nice and calm – boom! Out of nowhere, his greatest fear materialized. A big black bear was standing in the middle of the trail mere yards ahead of us. Obviously, all that drinking in and absorbing had made us pretty quiet, and since we were back on dirt and mud, there was no crunching of boots on gravel to warn the bear.

Gord's fear, live and in color, was staring him in the face. There were no "self-help" books here to help him confront this one. It probably would have been nice to have had one of those books tied onto the end of a stick to smack the bruin with – or would that just provoke him as some of those books provoke me? Stick, did I say stick? That's why we had carried these hockey sticks forty-five miles. He waved his at Yogi and yelled – all of this happening within about two seconds – and Mr. Bear took off. Like a big, black sofa bounding through the bushes, the bear disappeared into the rainforest like the morning mist. Gord turned around, as white as a ghost, as I arrived on the scene.

He stammered a few choice and non-Zen-like words: "Holy _____! Did you see that ____ing bear? I think he's gone now! Holy ____!" The adrenaline was still pumping, his heart thumping and breathing ragged, sweat beading on his forehead.

I'm sure we can draw all sorts of fuzzy metaphors, but my buddy had just stared down the thing he dreaded most. What a great example of confronting a lifelong fear and surviving. No, there was no huge Cecil B. DeMille movie scene, no physical clash on the field of battle – it was two very long seconds. Before that moment, there was anticipation, anxiety and dread – and afterward relief, victory and a smile.

Nervous laughter and the irony of the situation struck us – about an hour before the end of the trail on which we had endured hardship, pain, thirst, hunger and physical exhaustion, we'd been confronted by a bear within sight of the finish line. What a great headline or epitaph that would have made.

Well, the truth was, we'd both found what we sought – a chance at life, renewal, an opportunity to transcend beyond the ordinary by conquering something that existed only in our minds but was nonetheless absolutely real. A year later, and it strikes me again how much more powerful the fear we hold in our minds is than the actual physical danger when finally confronted.

That incident heightened our awareness as we moved forward over the last few miles toward the Parks Canada booth, the brass band, the champagne and the flyover by the Canadian Forces Snowbirds that surely awaited us – we were almost finished. We were sure they, whoever "they" were, would have prepared a triumphant reception: after all, we had prepared inspirational, yet appropriately humble speeches of "aw shucks" type gratitude.

There was still the odd ladder and bridge structure, but this was child's play compared to what we had already traversed. Just about 11 a.m. we came to a little bridge marked number 1. It didn't really cross anything but I think it was someone's great sense of humor to build it on the edge of the forest, in view of trail's end, and it provided a great opportunity to take each other's picture. We had done it!

Gord and I looked at each other, shook hands and wondered if anyone could possibly understand what we had just done. We had started out almost a year earlier in a coffee shop, created a dream and here we were realizing that dream in a way that only others who have done the same can truly appreciate.

We both expected more when we entered the Parks Canada office. Somebody or something that celebrated the accomplishment: not just us, but the 5,000 people who do this each summer should have some way of commemorating the achievement. I thought back to the dock at Nitinat Narrows, the T-shirts offered by the First Nations people, and my decision to wait until trail's end to purchase something – big mistake. There was nothing at trail's end! Brochures and maps, tide tables and some posters, a clerk and a pay phone were all we found.

We checked off the trail as our passes were perfunctorily stamped, and were pointed to the phone so we could contact Bamfield and order a taxi service to take us to town. This bit of anti-climactic bureaucracy performed, we headed out to the parking lot to await our ride.

We traded our disappointment about the reception as we lowered our backpacks and drained our water bottles. We didn't have to wait long for the van to show up, but long enough to feel some of the chill in the air. We threw our packs up into the back of the cargo hold and seated ourselves in the old-style, plush velour seats behind the driver. Wow, were they nice, in a seventies sort of way, compared to the log and rock seating we had not become accustomed to over the past week.

The ride into Bamfield was fast, even though we were on a gravel road; the driver seemed to take pleasure in reintroducing us to civilization as quickly as possible. Maybe that's what we were sensing at the trailhead office and now with the driver – this was employment for them: we'd had a unique life-altering experience, but they did this day after day…it was their means of livelihood. It was an adventure to us and a job to them. Our paradigms were different, to be sure.

We arrived in Bamfield and were deposited in a motel parking lot where the bus to Port Renfrew would pick us up in an hour or so. Across the street, we spotted a sign that said restaurant. That meant washrooms, too. Due to the aroma that we knew surrounded us, we expected to be asked to sit out in front of the eatery, on the outdoor patio's chairs. Instead, the waitress insisted we sit inside and leave our packs outside – she must have been used to the sights and smells of West Coast Trail hikers.

The thing I needed second most was breakfast, which I ordered before heading toward the washroom and heaven. Hot and cold running water and flush toilets – I promised myself never to take these things for granted again. I spent about fifteen minutes in the lap of luxury with real soap and paper towels and a white porcelain pony.

After a great meal, we loaded up with snacks, bottled water, etc. and boarded the bus for the three-hour ride back to Port Renfrew. There were several people boarding the bus, including the four women who had arrived at Michigan Creek late the night before. Their enthusiasm and energy had not waned one little bit. They decided that the bus driver looked like Kenny Rogers, and so led us in several songs as a tribute to the singer/bus driver. He seemed to respond with good humor as he told us a few tales about the drive we were embarking upon, logging roads and local lore.

The bus we were on had been purchased from the U.S. Navy and brought down from Alaska. It was built like an aircraft carrier, and probably needed to be in order to survive the roads we were on. Even though we were tired (or overstuffed from the restaurant) and drifted off to sleep from time to time, that ride was one of the trip's highlights. The beauty of the lakes, mountains and forests, and the magnificent remoteness of it all, combined to bring a kind of peace to the passengers. We settled in with our thoughts and enjoyed the spectacular views, the bumpy road, the afterglow of accomplishment, the hairpin turns and the last few minutes of wilderness before returning to civilization. I could feel the mix of anticipation and sorrow as we re-acclimated to what lay ahead and adjusted our internal clocks to human time from nature's time.

The driver dropped us off on the road in Port Renfrew in front of our car park area and we reclaimed the keys, thanked the proprietors for looking after the vehicle, loaded up, changed our boots and took off for Victoria. It was hard to believe that we had been here a week earlier to drop off the car. We had been so clean and excited – neophytes, still dry behind the ears.

One of the things we'd witnessed on that long ago day was a young man who had just completed the trail and was being attended to by his hiking companions. He had injured his leg and was in obvious pain. Naturally, this gave us cause for concern at the time as we wondered how we would fare, given our age and condition. Well, a week later, we had fared very well – the odd nick and scratch but no broken limbs, sprained ankles or cougar attacks. We had made it and were anxious to let our families know we had survived.

It was about 4 p.m., which meant that we would get into Victoria around dinner time and would need to find a motel. The drive to Victoria was fairly subdued, as we were both lost in our thoughts. I tried to seek out every viewpoint from the highway in order to hold on to the memory of the ocean, the giant trees, the waves, the coves, and what I felt was my real home. When I had lived in Victoria almost thirty years earlier, I'd bought an original painting of a surf shack located at the mouth of the Jordan River, north of Sooke. It still hangs in our home and as we passed the spot on the coast, I noticed that the shack was still there. Every time I look at that picture now, it revives the connection to that incredible week.

We found a motel on Gorge Road in Victoria and flipped a coin to see who would use the bathroom first. Gord won and I relaxed on the bed and watched an hour of television, and then we switched places. I had once lived just down the road from where this motel was located, and frequently used to go to the Keg for dinner. Gord indulged me and after shaves and showers, we headed downtown about 8 p.m. to enjoy dinner and drinks at my old haunt. The celebration was everything I expected: good food, wonderful view of the inner harbor and legislative buildings, a youthful electricity throughout the restaurant as people prepared to enjoy the Labor Day weekend.

A pleasant buzz from the bottle of cabernet sauvignon not only lowered my risk of heart disease but contributed to sleeping like a baby on an actual mattress. The next morning, we headed for Swartz Bay and managed to get on the first crossing to the mainland. We had breakfast on the ferry, Gord bought a souvenir for his grandson and soon we were making our way through the Lower Mainland and east to meet our wives at Gord and Brenda's cabin at Columbia Lake in the East Kootenays.

A long day of driving brought us back to reality as we viewed the still raging forest fires consuming so many acres of British Columbia. After what we had seen over the past week, it was a sad reminder of the fragility of our planet and our responsibility for conserving it.

## Afterward

The year since this trek has produced many additional journeys. These have been trips to places totally unfamiliar and in many ways exciting, unexpected and very fulfilling.

My wife, daughter and I drove home from the cabin at Columbia Lake on Labor Day through some heavily forested areas still smoldering from the forest fires of the previous few weeks. In places, we witnessed smoke and flame still evident at the roadside. Fire, one of the basic elements of life, presents the paradox of destruction on one hand and the inevitable renewal on the other. This seemed to reflect my own feelings about our week of adventure: I had gone through a baptismal fire that challenged me on every level, and had emerged into the light of possibility on those and more levels. I truly felt (and still do) that if I could accomplish the West Coast Trail, I could now consider the idea of taking on other, possibly bigger, challenges with an expectation of success. I knew this included not only physical endeavors but financial, spiritual and relationship growth, as well.

We seemed to have a number of visitors in the next few weeks who wanted to see the pictures, look at the maps and hear the stories. The storytelling seemed to fall to me, with editorial and humorous input from Gord. My mother-in-law was the first to suggest it, but many of our friends and family began to encourage me to write down my memories.

I don't know about your mother-in-law, but mine has always been one of my biggest supporters. When times were tough and she knew we were struggling, she always exhibited confidence and encouraged me, even when I couldn't see the possibilities for myself. She sensed abilities long dormant or ignored. Mary was also the first person to ask to read my writing efforts and her praise is largely responsible for me completing this project. She continues to be a major source of inspiration and comfort and for that, and her daughter, I remain forever grateful.

After spending the next Christmas in Regina with Leanne's family, I decided to take the Odyssey Program for the second time. That edition of the program began in January and ran for six months. Because I now had some familiarity and comfort with the process, this was, by far, the most powerful experience I've ever had with a program of inner growth. I began to speak out loud about writing a book. I started journaling most mornings, and realized that I had not been fulfilling my life's purpose with regard to career.

I have spent most of my life in some sort of sales-related job – no matter what the title was. I knew that this was never an expression of who I really was. Rather, it became the default position simply because I could do it. Any satisfaction was fleeting and success was always attached to the next commission check. As I delved deeper into myself through the Odyssey course, I began to see and feel the possibility of becoming more complete. Speaking about writing was a little like speaking about hiking the West Coast Trail. The more I did it, the more I began to believe that I could do it. Like talking about the hike before going, I was also setting myself up by telling others my dream. Writing this book has much in common with getting ready for the trail. It has been a journey in every sense of the word. The parallels between hiking and writing were revealed and supported through Odyssey as I continued many of the same techniques and disciplines to realize my goal.

My love affair with books began the evening my mother took me to the old public library building in Kitchener, Ontario. I was about eight years old and I can still vividly recall the smell of old books and wood shelves and floors combined with the solemn rule of absolute silence. That first library card, a handwritten piece of blue cardboard, was my passport to worlds I had never imagined to that point. I have been reading ever since, but now I marvel at how the process of writing also leads to discoveries, places and adventures only hinted at previously.

Someone asked me if I would still hike the West Coast Trail if I had read this book beforehand. What an interesting question. The answer is absolutely yes. Would I change some parts of it? Of course. I would allow more time to stop along the way, take lots more pictures, take an extra water bottle and more notes. My guess is that we all have a few West Coast Trails in us. It doesn't much matter whether it's forty-seven rugged miles of wilderness or the walk from the front door to the curb. If it challenges us, if it causes us to rethink our reason for being here, then it too is a journey worth taking. I don't think it matters where we start from, but rather, where we finish. My friend Howard expresses one of his goals as "finishing well," and that sounds like a pretty good idea to me. It doesn't matter where we've been, or even where we are now, but rather where we want to be.

I would recommend the West Coast Trail to anyone who is, or can become, fit enough to handle the physical rigors involved. It really does demonstrate the existence of a power greater than ourselves while showing how closely connected we are to that same power. Man can't create something this extraordinary – only borrow it for a short time and marvel at it, respect it and be grateful for it.

Good luck on the journey to your West Coast Trail.

Bob Bannon

November 2005

## Sources of Information and Inspiration

**Parks Canada**
www.parkscanada.gc.ca/
pacificrim
1-250-726-7721

**Soaring with the Eagles**
Christopher Alan Brawn
University of Calgary
ISBN 0-9695401-6-7

**Blisters and Bliss**
David Foster and
Wayne Aitken
B&B Publishing
Victoria, B.C.
ISBN 1-894384-65-2

**The Odyssey Program**
www.rebuildingcanada.com
attention: Howard Parsons
1-403-240-0045

**Mountain Equipment Co-Op**
830 10 Ave. SW
Calgary, Alberta

**Campers Village**
7208 Macleod Tr. SE
Calgary, Alberta

**People of the Southwest
Coast of Vancouver Island**
Scott, R. Bruce
Copyright 1974, R. Bruce Scott
1173 Hewlett Place
Victoria, B.C.

*Quote on page 1 from:*
**The Edge of the Sea**
by Carson, Rachel
Mifflin Co., Mass. 1955

**Contact Robert J. Bannon at: www.onestepoutings.com**